Chataway

Also available

Phoneme Factory
Developing Speech and Language Skills: A Resource for Teachers, Teaching Assistants and Therapists
Gwen Lancaster
ISBN10: 1-84312-382-7
ISBN13: 978-1-84312-382-8

Language for Learning
A Practical Guide for Supporting Children with Language and Communication Difficulties Across the Curriculum
Sue Hayden & Emma Jordan
ISBN10: 1-84312-468-8
ISBN13: 978-1-84312-468-9

Word Play
Language Activities for Children
Sheila Wolfendale & Trevor Bryans
ISBN10: 1-84312-439-4
ISBN13: 978-1-84312-439-9

Chataway

Making communication count from Foundation Stage to Key Stage Three

Andrew Burnett and
Jackie Wylie

Routledge
Taylor & Francis Group

LONDON AND NEW YORK

First published 2007
by Routledge
2 Park Square, Milton Park, Abingdon, Oxon, OX14 4RN

Simultaneously published in the USA and Canada
by Routledge
270 Madison Ave, New York, NY 10016

Routledge is an imprint of the Taylor & Francis Group, an informa business

Typeset in Bliss by RefineCatch Limited, Bungay, Suffolk
Printed and bound in Great Britain by Bell & Bain Ltd, Glasgow

British Library Cataloguing in Publication Data
A catalogue record for this book is available from the British Library

Library of Congress Cataloging in Publication Data
A catalog record has been requested for this book

ISBN10: 1–84312–438–6 (pbk)
ISBN13: 978–1–84312–438–2 (pbk)   # 134992212

Contents

Acknowledgements

For their consistent enthusiasm and support during the development and piloting of the Chataway materials, we would like to thank our colleagues and the children at:

Thornbury Primary School, Plymouth
Laira Green Primary School, Plymouth
Estover Community College (Enhanced Specialist Provision), Plymouth

plus the many colleagues and children in other settings who have indirectly contributed to the development of Chataway over the years.

We would like to thank Liz Robbins for her detailed feedback about, and suggestions for improving, the final drafts, and Mark Masidlover for his interest in the Chataway project and kind permission to quote from the Derbyshire Language Scheme.

Permission for references to and quotes from the Bristol Language Development Scales has been kindly granted by publishers NFER-Nelson.

Introduction

Developing oral language skills

Oral language skills are something that most of us take for granted.

We assume that children will automatically pick up the rules and social conventions related to these core skills, and most of them do. They learn language first from their family and later from people they meet every day – at home, in their education settings and out in the wider world.

Spoken language involves the development of complex skills. A competent conversationalist will be able automatically to adjust their use of language to suit the context and the people they are with, altering their conversational style to take account of differing communication demands. For example, answering questions in a formal situation (e.g. in the classroom) will be handled in a very different way from responding to friends in the school playground.

When we look more closely at the complexity of interaction and communication, it is amazing to think that in most instances we develop oral language skills without ever having to consciously think about them. For a significant number of young people, however, acquiring these skills is a real challenge. Indeed there are many adults who may cope generally, but who find at least some conversational and related social skills a continuing challenge throughout their lives.

So, if these skills are so important, how can we help children who struggle with learning them?

Chataway

We have attempted to address this question by producing Chataway. This is an approach initially based on, and inspired by, a Bristol University research project undertaken with families in the Bristol area during the 1970s. The research team undertook a longitudinal study of children from 150 families, recording, analysing and then categorising the language developed and used by the children from age 15 months to 5 years. Following completion of the project, the team published the Bristol Language Development Scales or 'BLADES' (Gutfreund et al, 1989). The scales analysed children's use of language under three main headings:

- Semantics (the meaning)
- Syntax (the grammar)
- Pragmatics (the functional understanding and use of language).

Chataway is concerned with *pragmatics*, namely the understanding and use of core functional language skills:

> The function of an utterance is the purpose which it serves in conversation. Among other things, we talk to control the speech or actions of others, to exchange information, to express feelings and attitudes or ask about those of others and to facilitate the channel of communication itself. More specifically, we may, for example, command, suggest, explain, threaten, ask for clarification, express feelings or give a factual piece of information.

Gutfreund et al, 1989: 7

We simplified and condensed the original BLADES material so that practitioners would find the approach more accessible and flexible, and we added a bank of activities for use in language groups in Key Stage 1 and Key Stage 2 settings. These activities were used to address the language needs of pupils in two primary schools in the Plymouth area and our education colleagues provided much useful feedback. We then differentiated many of the activities for use in Key Stage 3, and again piloted them. In addition, drawing on our extensive experience of working with children at the Foundation Stage, we extended the activities to cover the needs of younger children. **This means that we can confidently recommend the Chataway approach for use with students across the full educational age range.**

Chataway focuses on forty basic 'use of language' functions and systematically embeds their naturalistic use in group work activities. (Details of the content of the Chataway materials and approach are outlined in Chapter 1.) We have also included an option to target two categories of functional language in more detail – questions and negatives – based on the developmental progression outlined in the Derbyshire Language Scheme (DLS). (See Chapter 4.) We consider that the DLS approach corresponds well with our experience of the usual patterns of children's language development in these two areas.

Although we have not used or directly referred to their work, we also acknowledge the importance of texts by Joan Tough (author of several books, including *A Place for Talk*) and Ann Locke and Maggie Beech (*Teaching Talking*).

The Chataway approach

Users of our materials should note that the Chataway approach does not target the student's vocabulary knowledge or usage, nor their development of grammar. Whilst we would always recommend modelling appropriate grammar and vocabulary usage, the children's attempts are always accepted. Chataway targets the children's functional and successful use of whatever core language skills they currently have.

To illustrate this further, in some Activity Sheets we have included examples of acceptable responses which are not grammatically correct but which, nevertheless, demonstrate that the child is using the target language successfully: for example, 'to express inability' → 'He no fly' (He can't fly).

Practitioners and parents are encouraged not to correct or directly work on vocabulary and grammar and, because children can make progress even if they currently use limited or immature vocabulary or grammatical forms, they usually respond enthusiastically to the functional 'accepting' approach we have developed here.

In Chataway we draw attention to a number of vital language skills which are often overlooked and target these through the use of specific strategies. Examples of these skills include 'Persist in Call' and 'Request Clarification', as well as social language skills such as 'Challenge' and 'Encourage'.

The focus of much current language teaching is relatively restricted, tending to target the more familiar and more formal core language skills, such as question and answer, naming, giving explanations, giving and receiving instructions and so on, but Chataway targets the full range of functional language skills.

There has been an increasing focus in education on 'thinking and reasoning' skills, which rely on the secure development of the core language skills targeted by the Chataway approach.

The National Curriculum

Many of the skills covered in Chataway are implicit in the Speaking and Listening Curriculum, but the understanding and use of these skills is not appropriately assessed and taught for all children. We believe that the advice included in *Speaking, Listening, Learning: working with children in Key Stages 1 and 2* (QCA, 2003) makes the assumption that children will automatically use language skills if it is expected of them, but many cannot do this.

The teaching objectives outlined by the QCA are dependent on the child having already developed high level oral language skills. For example, they anticipate that in Year 1 pupils will be able to 'decide how to report a group's views' and in Year 2, 'listen to each other's views and preferences, agree the next steps to take and identify contributions by each group member'.

Needless to say, the demands are significantly greater for older students. All the QCA teaching objectives include complex and demanding tasks, and assume the ready use of highly sophisticated language skills. They are expected to be 'built into teaching and learning' in schools but little or no advice is given about how to ensure that students can understand, practise and readily apply such advanced skills – or indeed ensure that they will have a functional repertoire of core language skills.

The Chataway approach addresses this lack of guidance and includes assessment and intervention for a wide range of core language skills including:

- the exchange of information
- expressing feelings and attitudes
- controlling others and obtaining information about their needs
- maintaining and developing social relationships.

For further information about how Chataway relates to the teaching objectives in the Speaking and Listening Curriculum, refer to Chapter 3.

What does the Chataway approach offer?

Chataway enables practitioners to teach and establish:

- an extensive range of core language skills (40 functional language categories plus additional optional differentiation for the development and use of questions and negatives)
- strategies for learning and socialisation (e.g. seeking clarification, check to confirm, encourage, express approval)
- important, but sometimes overlooked, language skills (such as 'Persist in Call'), that less successful learners often do not use.

Chataway provides a number of further practical benefits to education practitioners:

- The activities require minimal levels of resources, or rely on resources that are easily accessed, for example playing cards;
- Photocopiable resources are provided;
- Information on sources of some useful, low-cost published resources.

In summary, the Chataway approach includes the following key features:

- Evidence-informed ideas for intervention based on the normal development of functional language skills;
- A screening assessment to help practitioners identify children suitable for different levels of work;
- An intervention approach suitable for group work and enabling groups to cover a range of general ability;
- Adaptations suggested for different age groups/Key Stages;
- A clear focus on functional use of language, whatever the level of the children's current vocabulary and grammar skills;
- 54 Activity Sheets, covering a wide range of basic, functional language skills and cross-referenced to Progress Record Sheets, an Activity Index and recommendations regarding suitability for different age groups;
- Activities that can be used by a range of practitioners with no specialist knowledge and incorporating both cooperative and competitive activities;
- Advice on the use of a range of strategies that will enhance the children's skills and learning during Chataway activities, as well as in the wider education environment or at home;
- Cross-referencing to curricular objectives.

NOTE: Pages with a ▤ can be photocopied for use in the classroom.

CHAPTER 1

How to use Chataway

Which children will benefit from using the Chataway approach?

In some cases this will be an easy decision – the children will have few functional pragmatic language skills when they try to interact with others around them, even if they have some basic expressive language. Such children will use the language skills they have for a very limited range of purposes, for example you may note that they use language mostly to label and request things and do not ask questions or give clarification, etc.

Other children may communicate at a generally functional level, particularly with same-age peers, but will struggle to manage beyond simple conversational exchanges, in class or social settings, or within larger groups.

A third category of children might include those who struggle to manage even basic everyday exchanges and interactions and who may well display frustration or distress caused by social barriers or isolation.

Children with these limited skill levels need to learn to use language effectively in a wide range of situations, including one-to-one conversations; small groups; the classroom; other environments such as home, the playground, drama groups, after-school clubs, 'out and about', etc.

Chataway is designed to develop oral language skills through group work and to promote their subsequent use in a range of everyday settings. Practitioners can run groups that include children at different levels of functional language skill development – you may just need to support some children more consistently.

Some children may be starting to learn the targeted skill while others in the group may be generalising the use of the skill – these latter children can act as models for the beginners. Children usually learn from their peers very effectively and this process can be readily encouraged within systematic group work.

The Chataway approach

The Chataway approach enables the practitioner to:

- **quickly identify the children's current skills and targets**: screening assessment and ongoing Progress Record entries

- **allocate children to skills activity groups**: these groups can be adjusted if children need to work at a more basic or advanced level (mixed ability groups can be very effective)

- **select activities** that will address areas of need and also suit the children's interests and their familiar daily experiences

- **promote functional oral language skills in the classroom and other environments**, using the Chataway records and developmental reference notes.

Colleagues can be readily briefed about current targets for children so that these can be promoted consistently. For example, in a topic-based activity a child might be prompted to give instructions to the rest of the group, or, during science lessons a child might be prompted to give an explanation in response to What? or When? questions.

Getting started

Let's consider a likely situation.

You have half a dozen children in the class who struggle with understanding and using basic language skills, working with peers, socialising, responding to adults and other children. Time to act!

1 The screening assessment

Get someone who knows the child to fill in the screening assessment form – this will only take a few minutes. The screening assessment asks if the child uses language for a specific number of purposes, such as asking and answering WH (what, where, when, who) questions. For ease and speed of application only a limited number of Chataway targets are included in this screening. These targets are easy to identify and are likely to be representative of the child's general pragmatic abilities.

The rating scale – 'often → sometimes → rarely → never' means that if the test is re-administered (following group work and generalisation), any progress that the child has made can be identified. Information from the screening assessment can be used to start a Progress Record entry for each child, referring to the Examples Table as required. (See Chapter 4.)

2 The Progress Record: ongoing assessment plus recording

In the Progress Record the targeted language skills are set out in normal developmental order. (This order is based on information derived from the Bristol Language Developmental Scales, the Derbyshire Language Scheme, other texts and research, and the extensive teaching and therapy experience of the two authors.) Skills are categorised across ten levels. Level 1 covers the earliest developmental language, for example skills such as 'Express Wants', and Level 10 includes skills at a higher level of development, for example 'Challenge'.

We recommend the following straightforward method, which allows you to keep ongoing records that can be referred to when planning and reviewing IEPs, discussing progress with parents and colleagues and deciding which targets to select.

On the Progress Record:

- Single examples of using a skill can be marked in the column for each child, using / ;

- Where children use the skill a few times, record it as ///////;

- Continuing use of the skills, to include some generalisation to other situations can be represented by cross-hatching XXXXX;

- Established use of the target skill is shown by blocking in the space on the record;

- If you want to demonstrate change over time, you can use different colour recording, for example to record progress in each school term – this also allows you to keep meaningful records for newer members in the groups.

Level	Target	John	Fred	Karen
2	Make Statement	/////////////	XXXXXXXXX	///////////
3	Express Feelings			XXXXXXXXX
4	State Intention	XXXXXXXXXX	//////////	
5	Give Explanation			//////////

3 Selecting targets

The Chataway targets are arranged in developmental order and so, initially, you are likely to need to assess for skills listed at the earlier levels, in order to ensure that there are no significant gaps in the children's profiles. Although your selected children may need to be taught to understand and use some, or even many of these skills, they probably *won't* have to slavishly work through *all* of the Chataway levels.

In practice, whatever their current level of language ability, children will often have to cope with understanding, and even trying to use, higher level skills during their daily experience. For example, if a child is involved in a playground incident, staff will probably ask them 'What happened?' These are opportunities for you to note how the child copes and to plan for appropriate teaching activities if they struggle to understand and effectively communicate their knowledge and needs.

To select activities that target a particular skill, refer to the Activities Index. This will direct you to several activities that target that skill. You can check on the suitability of these activities for use with your children by referring to the Activities by Age Index. This index is provided to assist your selection, but your decision may depend on your knowledge of the children. You can, of course, adjust individual activity details to suit, or simply go for it and experiment.

What counts as successful use of a skill?

As we suggested in the introduction to Chataway, basic functional language skills can be used effectively even where the speaker has quite limited vocabulary or grammar. For example if a child says 'What doing?' you, as a native speaker, know that they are using a developmentally delayed form of the question 'What are you doing?' The context of an activity will also often help listeners understand the intention of even very limited language – think of your own experiences of trying to communicate when you are abroad!

REMEMBER

Chataway is about targeting and teaching effective functional language skills.

While it is constructive to model the correct grammar and vocabulary during conversations and activities, we recommend that you do not highlight or directly work on the grammatical or vocabulary errors/immaturities in the language used by the children.

What if I need to do more work on a particular target?

In the Activities Index we have indicated all the activity sheets that can be used to teach and promote specific language targets.

You can also develop your own ideas about when and where a target can be promoted – this is all about generalisation and once you start you won't stop. *You* know your children best and are best placed to identify teaching opportunities. From our experience, practitioners frequently adapt activities to suit their own children and working environments. The development of this feeling of 'ownership' is always positive.

It is likely that for some targets children will need to work on using the language in several different contexts before they begin to successfully generalise its use. They may also enjoy repeating the activities. We have endeavoured to make activities intrinsically enjoyable and so repetition is not usually a problem. (If you want to try out other published activities, refer to Resources and Bibliography.)

What about targets with only a few activities listed?

Some targets don't readily lend themselves to specific activities, but they *can* successfully be worked on indirectly – an example of this is the target 'Persist in Call'. (Refer to Chapter 2, 'General Strategies', for more ideas.)

How can I lead a group activity and simultaneously record the children's language?

Ideally two adults run the groups, with one responsible for recording use of language.

Working alone, it is possible to keep a limited record of significant language use in a small notebook, or use a tick list for targets and names. It is best to record information as soon as possible after the group.

During many activities it is possible to encourage children to take the lead, or to discuss their proposed actions with their team mates, allowing time to observe and record language.

What is the best way to plan groups?

Ideally, teacher and teaching assistant will be planning together on a regular basis, with occasional input from parents and Speech and Language Therapy colleagues whenever this is possible.

Once you are familiar with the Chataway approach and Chataway resources, you will feel confident enough to select from Chataway to suit your particular needs.

Initially you may wish to adopt a more systematic Chataway approach which, following initial assessment and grouping, is likely to include the following steps:

- Look at the current Progress Record levels recorded for the children;
- Select one or more targets suitable for current group work;
- Refer to the Activities Index and select appropriate activities;
- If required, check the Activities by Age Index;
- Write a Group Plan;
- Arrange any resources needed for the activities.

During the session:

- Keep a record of any relevant language use, to include new language not currently targeted.

After the session:

- Enter new information in the group Progress Record and any relevant observations about activity suitability, group responses, etc.;
- Plan the next group session – for consolidation/generalisation or a new target as appropriate.

> ## REMEMBER
>
> Don't focus on the children's vocabulary or general grammar skills – just model correct usage.

And finally, plan the group sessions to suit the children's ages, attention spans and interests. It is often productive to follow a table-top activity with a more active task, for example. Don't worry about using an activity more than once – the activities are designed to be fun as well as instructive and you will find that children will ask to 'play' them again – 'Sharks' is a good example of this.

Group Plans

Here are two sample Group Plans (consecutive weeks) that were used with children in an established Key Stage 2 group.

'Chataway' Group Plan 1

Group Key Stage 2	*Date* Week 6/Term 2	*Leader* AB

Resources

Warm up	Activity 52 'How Many Benny?' – Cards with numbers written on
Activity 1	Activity 8 'Make Me Happy' – 'Happy Families' cards
Activity 2	Activity 10 'Memory Magic' – None

Other notes

Warm up

Continued from previous session on request – limit number of turns as 'warm up' only

Target language – **Ask How Many? Question** e.g. '**How many** have I got?'

Activity 1

Target language – **Make Condition** e.g. 'If you give us Mr Chop, we'll give you Master Chalk'

Apologise e.g. 'Sorry, we haven't got that'

Activity 2 (if longer session planned)

Target language (Use of Strategies – discuss value with group first)

Request Repetition e.g. 'Say it again please'

Check to Confirm e.g. 'Did you say 7–3–4?'

Review of session

Discuss success and value of using strategies in 'Memory Magic'

Planning for next session

Share plan for Activity 43 'Guided Walk'

What obstacles and other equipment do group suggest we use? (Make Suggestion + Agree/Disagree could be promoted here)

'Chataway' Group Plan 2

Group Key Stage 2	Date Week 7/Term 2	Leader AB

Resources

Warm up No – due to Guided Walk time factor

Activity 1 Activity 10 'Memory Magic' – none

Activity 2 Activity 43 'Guided Walk' – obstacles + boxes chosen last week

Other notes Book School Hall + leave items there at break

Warm up

Not today

Activity 1

Complete turns – activity started last week. Extend to 4 items to remember &
1–2 children to take turn as leader

Activity 2

2 teams – though explain it's not a race. Award bonus points for not bumping into
obstacles, + good instructions.

Language targets:

Direct Request e.g. 'Go forward five steps'

Encourage e.g. 'Keep going'

Review of session

e.g. discuss who managed to follow the directions best and did so w/o bumping into
the obstacles.

Promote '*Approval*' e.g. 'That was brilliant Ben'

Group to shake hands with one other person and say 'well done'

Planning for next session

Group discussion and vote to select one of our favourite activities

Select 2nd activity –? Activity 45 'When Do You Do It?'

CHAPTER 2

General strategies

Each Chataway activity has identified learning goals which correspond to particular language development categories. There are, however, some categories for which we have *not* included specific activities: these involve more general conversational skills which can be developed and supported during daily school routine as well as in specific group sessions. These categories are as follows:

Greeting
For example 'Hello', 'Alright!', 'Bye'.

- Use structured group activities and in class daily routine to support greetings between the children, e.g. starting and ending sessions with simple 'hello' or 'goodbye' activities.

- For younger children saying hello or goodbye to a class pet/puppet/popular visitor, etc. may be helpful in promoting and reinforcing this conversational habit.

Call/Persist in Call
Calling to get another person's attention, e.g. 'Mum!', 'Hey!' and continuing to try to get attention when you get no response at first.

- During group activities encourage the children to say the name of the person they are talking to before they ask their question.

- During daily school routine talk about how important it is to get another person's attention before speaking to them – link this to the importance of other listening skills such as sitting still, looking at the person who is talking and thinking about the words that someone is saying. For more information on 'Active Listening' refer to *Functional Language in the Classroom* by Maggie Johnson (2005).

- If necessary use a puppet (younger children) or role play (older students) to model how 'calling' and 'persisting' can be effective when interacting with another person.

Response to Call
Showing that the speaker is listening and is available to take part in conversation, e.g. 'Yes?', 'What!'.

- During group activities remind and encourage the children to respond to someone calling their name or trying to get their attention.
- Role play if helpful. To avoid possible embarrassment use two puppets, seeing who can act out the most amusing exchange.
- As a group, talk about how making such responses helps people know that you are listening and encourages them to continue talking to and working/playing with you.

Request Repetition
Asking for repetition where the previous utterance by the listener has not been heard or understood, e.g. 'What did you say?'.

- Encourage children to ask the speaker to say something again if they clearly have not heard or understood – for younger children a 'Mr Mumble' role play can help with understanding this concept.
- Talk about how it helps us remember if we hear things twice. Some specific activities can be used to focus on this, e.g. 10 Memory Magic.

Request Permission
For example 'Can I put the telly on?', 'Me go wee?'.

- During group activities and in the classroom encourage the children to verbalise their wishes and needs in any way they are able to do so. Give positive re-enforcement when children request permission, e.g. 'That was really nice asking Sam. Well done'.

Offer
Offer to do or give something, e.g. 'Want me to help you?', 'Have a crisp'.

- Encourage the children to offer to help each other when they are stuck. The non-competitive and 'team' nature of many activities in Chataway will help children learn to work together in this way.
- Use snacks time, etc. to allow practise of this skill – the chosen student might then have to 'offer' a crisp or healthy snack or drink to 30+ children.

Give Clarification

Re-words something for others to understand or answers a direct request for clarification, e.g. 'The one on the table' → 'Eh'??? → 'The big blue one on the table'.

- Again, some specific 'Chataway' activities could be used to encourage this skill, e.g. 41 Tell Me What To Do, 42 Ask Me What To Do.

- It is often very difficult for children to develop awareness of the needs of the listener in this way and frequent modelling and positive feedback will be needed.

Request Clarification

Asks for the other speaker to clarify what has been said – e.g. 'What do you mean?' 'This book?'.

- Children need to learn that even adults sometimes give instructions which are lacking important information. Children need to be encouraged in the classroom to request further information to help them process what has been said. Praise them for asking relevant questions to clarify what has been said and acknowledge when you have not given enough information, e.g. 'You're right, I didn't tell you *where* to put it did I!'

- Some Chataway activities could be used to work specifically on this area, e.g. 11 Which One Do You Mean?.

- Children particularly enjoy 'silly' consequences of insufficient information. You can model this by encouraging the children to tell you what to do during a simple activity (such as making a sandwich). When they give incomplete information (e.g. 'Put it on top') point this out by making a silly suggestion (e.g. 'Where? On top of my head?'). Using a puppet who responds very literally can be a useful way of demonstrating this.

Check to Confirm

A repetition of the other person's previous utterance with rising intonation to check that it has been heard or understood correctly, e.g. 'It's downstairs' → 'Downstairs?'.

- It is important to emphasise to the children during all Chataway activities that they can check to make sure they have heard or understood correctly before responding.

- Some Chataway activities could be used to specifically encourage this skill, e.g. 10 Memory Magic, 41 Tell Me What To Do.

- Checking to confirm is also a skill which needs to be encouraged in the classroom, out of structured group activities. Give positive re-enforcement when children use this strategy to help them understand, e.g. 'Well done Sam – you checked you heard it right didn't you! And now you definitely know what to do in our science task'.

Evasion

Delaying or avoiding acting on an instruction or answering a question, e.g. 'Put your book away' → 'In a minute', 'Who did that?' → 'I don't know'.

- Although this can be quite a negative skill, particularly when you are trying to encourage children to answer questions or follow instructions in class, it is also a useful social strategy which children need to develop.

- You could recommend and encourage the strategy where for example children have to undertake several tasks and are currently busy, e.g. pouring a liquid (so putting the book away will have to wait).

Promise

For example 'I promise I'll . . .' 'I will do it'.

- Model this in class, for example, promising certainties such as 'I promise we will go out to play once this is finished'.

- Promises can be modelled through drama and literacy, e.g. discussing how characters have made/kept or broken promises and the impact of this on others.

- Children could be encouraged to make promises in the context of the school day, for example, promising that they will do their homework – or promising to bring in items for news rounds, topic work, etc.

Apologise

- This is a positive social skill which is actively encouraged at home and at school.

- During Chataway activities children can be encouraged to use apology, e.g. when asked for a card that they don't have, 'I'm sorry I can't help you!' – from experience the children rather like this phrase, often with a rather mischievous intent which is safe – 'it's only a game'.

Accessing the Speaking and Listening Curriculum

The following tables link relevant teaching objectives from *Speaking, Listening, Learning: working with children in Key Stages 1 and 2* (QCA, 2003) to Chataway targets.

Table 3.1

Year/Term	Strand	Teaching Objective	Chataway targets
Year 1 Term 1	Speaking	1. To describe incidents or tell stories from their own experience in an audible voice	Make Statement Express Feelings Express Attitudes Give Explanation Give Clarification
Year 1 Term 1	Group discussion and interaction	3. To ask and answer questions, make relevant contributions, offer suggestions and take turns	Ask/Answer Wh Questions Ask Yes/No Questions Make Statement Express Feelings Express Attitude Ask about Feelings Ask about Attitude Make Suggestion Encourage Give Explanation Give Clarification Request Repetition Request Explanation Request Clarification
Year 1 Term 2	Listening	6. To listen and follow instructions accurately, asking for help and clarification if necessary	Request Repetition Request Explanation Request Clarification Check to Confirm
Year 1 Term 2	Group discussion and interaction	7. To take turns to speak, listen to other's suggestions and talk about what they are going to do	Refuse or Disagree Agree Make Suggestion Encourage Express Approval Express Disapproval
Year 1 Term 3	Listening	10. To listen to tapes or videos and express views about how a story or information has been presented	Express Feelings Express Attitude
Year 1 Term 3	Group discussion and interaction	11. To explain their views to others in a small group and decide how to report the group's views to the class	Give Explanation Express Approval Express Disapproval
Year 1 Term 3	Drama	12. To discuss why they like a performance	Ask/Answer Wh Questions Express Approval Express Attitude Express Feelings

Table 3.2

Year/Term	Strand	Teaching Objective	Chataway targets
Year 2 Term 1	Listening	14. To listen to others in class, ask relevant questions and follow instructions	Ask/Answer Wh Questions Request Repetition Request Clarification Request Explanation Check to Confirm
Year 2 Term 1	Group discussion and interaction	15. To listen to each other's views and preferences, agree the next steps and identify contributions by each group member	Ask about Wants Ask about Intentions Encourage Express Feelings Express Attitude Make Generalisation
Year 2 Term 2	Group discussion and interaction	19. To ensure everyone contributes, allocate tasks, consider alternatives and reach agreement	Ask/Answer Wh Questions Ask about Wants Ask about Intentions Ask Yes/No Questions Encourage Ask about Feelings Ask about Attitude Make Suggestion Refuse/Disagree Agree Express Approval Express Disapproval
Year 2 Term 3	Speaking	21. To use language and gesture to support the use of models/diagrams/displays when explaining	Give Explanation
Year 2 Term 3	Group discussion and interaction	23. To work effectively in groups by ensuring each group member takes a turn, challenging, supporting and moving on	Refuse/Disagree Agree Encourage Challenge/Respond to Challenge Express Approval Express Disapproval

Table 3.3

Year/Term	Strand	Teaching Objective	Chataway targets
Year 3 Term 1	Speaking	25. To explain a process or present information, ensuring items are clearly sequenced, relevant details are included and accounts ended effectively	Give Explanation Give Clarification
Year 3 Term 1	Listening	26. To follow up other's points and show whether they agree or disagree in a whole class discussion	Refuse/Disagree Agree Request Repetition Request Clarification Express Approval Express Disapproval
Year 3 Term 1	Group discussion and interaction	27. To use talk to organise roles and action	Refuse/Disagree Agree Make Suggestion
Year 3 Term 2	Group discussion and interaction	31. To actively include and respond to all members of the group	Ask/Answer Wh Questions Request Repetition Request Explanation Request Clarification Ask about Wants Ask about Intentions Ask about Feelings Ask about Attitude Encourage Give Explanation Give Clarification Express Wants Express Intentions Express Feelings Express Attitude
Year 3 Term 3	Speaking	33. To sustain conversation, explaining or giving reasons for their views or choices	Give Explanation Express Feelings Express Attitude Give Clarification Express Approval Express Disapproval
Year 3 Term 3	Group discussion and interaction	35. To use the language of possibility to investigate and reflect on feelings, behaviour or relationships	Express Feelings Express Attitude Make Suggestion Request Explanation Give Explanation Ask/Answer Wh Questions

Table 3.4

Year/Term	Strand	Teaching Objective	Chataway targets
Year 4 Term 1	Speaking	37. To use and reflect on some ground rules for dialogue	Give Explanation Give Clarification Request Repetition Request Explanation Request Clarification
Year 4 Term 1	Group discussion and interaction	39. To take different roles in groups and use language appropriate to them, including roles of leader, reporter, scribe and mentor	Direct Request Ask Wh Questions Request Repetition State Intention Give Explanation Make Suggestion Give Clarification Encourage Make Generalisation Check to Confirm Challenge
Year 4 Term 2	Speaking	41. To respond appropriately to the contributions of others in the light of alternative viewpoints	Express Feelings Express Attitude Give Explanation Give Clarification Make Suggestion Express Approval Express Disapproval
Year 4 Term 3	Drama	47. To create roles showing how behaviour can be interpreted from different viewpoints	Express Feelings Express Attitudes Ask/Answer Wh Questions Request Explanation Give Explanation

Table 3.5

Year/Term	Strand	Teaching Objective	Chataway targets
Year 5 Term 1	Listening	49. To identify some aspects of talk which vary between formal and informal occasions	Greeting Ask/Answer Wh Questions Agree Disagree Express Approval Express Disapproval
Year 5 Term 2	Listening	52. To identify different questions types and evaluate impact on audience	Ask Yes/No Questions Ask Wh Questions Answer Wh Questions
Year 5 Term 2	Group discussion and interaction	53. To understand and use the processes and language of decision-making	Agree Disagree Challenge/Respond to Challenge Make Generalisation
Year 5 Term 3	Speaking	55. To present a spoken argument, sequencing points logically, defending views with evidence and making use of persuasive language	Make Statement Ask/Answer Wh Questions Request Explanation Give Explanation Give Clarification
Year 5 Term 3	Group discussion and interaction	56. To understand different ways to take the lead and support others in groups	Ask Wh Questions Ask about Wants Ask about Feelings Ask about Attitude State Intention Make Suggestion Encourage

Table 3.6

Year/Term	Strand	Teaching Objective	Chataway targets
Year 6 Term 1	Group discussion and interaction	60. To understand and use a variety of ways to criticise constructively and respond to criticism	Express Disapproval/Criticise Request Clarification Give Clarification
Year 6 Term 2	Speaking	62. To participate in a whole-class debate using the conventions and language of debate, including standard English	Encourage Ask/Answer Wh Questions Agree Refuse or Disagree Express Approval Express Disapproval
Year 6 Term 2	Group discussion and interaction	63. To consider examples of conflict and resolution, exploring language used	Agree Refuse or Disagree Request Explanation Make Generalisation Challenge/Respond to Challenge
Year 6 Term 3	Group discussion and interaction	66. To identify the ways spoken language varies according to differences in context and purpose of use	Request Explanation Give Explanation Make Statement Make Suggestion

CHAPTER 4

Assessment, planning and recording

Screening assessment

Tick one of the four headings for each skill area. Remember that you are assessing what the child is using language to do rather than their knowledge of grammar. If the child makes grammatical errors but it is clear they are using language for the purposes outlined below then they should not be marked down for incorrect grammar.

This screening assessment is a photocopiable resource.

The child can . . .	Often	Sometimes	Rarely	Never
Express Feelings (e.g. 'I'm angry', 'I feel sick' etc.)				
Express Attitudes (e.g. I not like that', 'That nice' etc.)				
Ask for Repetition when they don't understand/can't remember what you have said (e.g. 'What was that?', 'Can you say that again?' etc.)				
Ask for Clarification when they don't understand (e.g. 'Do you mean the big one or the little one?', 'This one?','What do you mean?' etc.)				
Ask Wh Questions (What? Where? Who? When?)				
Answer Wh Questions (What? Where? Who? When?)				
Give Explanations incl. Answer How? & What for? Questions (e.g. How did you find this? → 'I look in the big one')				
Give Clarification when requested to do so (e.g. do you mean this one? → 'Yes, I do')				
State Intention (e.g. 'I'm going swimming today') – note: this is not in reply to a question, 'What are you going to do?' but is a comment made spontaneously by the child				
Make Suggestion (e.g. 'Let's go outside', 'Shall we play chase?' etc.)				
Express Approval/Disapproval (e.g. 'Good!', 'That silly!' etc.)				
Request Explanation i.e. asks 'How?' and 'What for?' questions				
Make Condition ('If it stops raining we'll go out', 'I'll give you one if you . . .'				

Chataway © Andrew Burnett and Jackie Wylie, Routledge, 2007

Examples table

Level	Functions	Examples
1	Call	'Mum!' 'Hey!' 'Oy!' 'Miss!'
1	Express Wants	(May be one word only) 'Up' 'More milk' 'Want watch telly'
2	Direct Request or Command	'Give me that car' 'Shut the door'
2	Refuse or Disagree	Open the door please → 'No!' It my car! → 'No!!'
2	Agree	Will you shut the door? → 'Yes' That's a big one → 'Yes'
2	Make Statement	'There's a dog in the garden' 'Me got car'
3	Express Feelings	'I feel poorly sick' 'I am very cross now!'
3	Express Attitudes	'I not like that' 'I don't like homework'
3	Ask Wh Questions (not How? Why? or What for?)	'Where ball?'　'What you doing?' 'Which one?'　'Who is next?' 'Who that?'　'When . . .?'
3–7	Answer Wh Questions (not How? Why? or What for?	Where Daddy? → 'In bed' What's this? → 'My car' Who's next? → 'Me!' When? → 'Now!'
4	Greetings	'Hello' 'Alright?!!' 'Ta-ta' 'Bye!'
4	Persist in Call	(Where someone has spoken and is continuing to try to get attention) 'Mummy' (no response) → 'Mummy!!'
4	Request Repetition	(When speaker has not been heard or understood properly) 'Pardon?' 'What?' 'Eh?'
4	State Intention	A statement of intention to do something (Not a reply to the question – what are you going to do?) 'I'm going school today' 'I (gonna) get it'
5	Request Permission	'Can I put telly on?' 'Me go wee?'
5	Prohibition	'Don't do that' 'Stop it!'
5	Give Explanation	Why . . .? → 'Cos I don't like them' How . . .? → 'You have to hold this so it won't come off' What . . . for? → 'To make it go faster!'
6	Ask about Wants	What you want for tea?'
6	Ask about Intentions	'What you gonna do?' 'You gonna play with me?'

Level	Functions	Examples
6	Offer	'(*Offer to do or give something*) 'I'll do it for you' 'Have a crisp'
6	Make Suggestion	'Lets go in the garden' 'Shall we play lego?'
6	Ask Yes/No Questions	Any question that can be answered 'yes' or 'no' 'Do you like sausages?' 'Isn't he silly'
6/7	Give Clarification	Clarification of speaker's previous utterance in response to a request for clarification Do you mean this one? → 'Yes I do'
7	Encourage	(. . . someone to do something) 'Go on!' 'That's right!' 'You can do it!'
7	Request Explanation (Why? How? and What for?)	'Why did you hit him?' 'What's that for?' 'How do I open this?'
7	Ask about Feelings	'Are you cross?' 'Do you feel happier now?'
7	Ask about Attitude	'Do you like singing?' 'Do you think he's a good goalie?'
7/8	Respond to Call	Showing that the speaker is listening and is available to take part in a conversation Daniel! → 'Yes?' 'What?!' 'Uh!'
7/8	Request Clarification	Request for the other speaker to clarify what has been said 'What do you mean?' '*This* book???'
8	Make Generalisation	'You mustn't play in the road' 'You must wash hands after the toilet'
8/9	Check to Confirm	(A repetition of the other person's previous utterance with rising intonation to check that it has been heard or understood properly) It's downstairs → 'Downstairs?'
9	Give Warning	'Look out!' 'Be careful!'
9	Evasion	Go and clean your teeth! → 'In a minute' Who did that? → 'I don't know'
9	Permit	'You can have mine' 'You can go first'
9/10	Promise	'I promise I'll . . .' 'I *will* do it!'
9/10	Challenge (+ Respond to Challenge)	To establish status – often in talk with peers 'I've got 2 cars' → 'Well I've got 10!' 'Mine's bigger than yours!'
10	Make Condition	'If it stops raining we'll go out' 'I'll give you one if you . . .'
10	Apologise	'Sorry' 'Excuse me' 'Pardon me!'
10	Express Approval	'Good idea!' 'Well done!'
10	Express Disapproval or Criticise	'That's naughty' 'That's silly' 'You done it wrong!'

Activity index

Level	Function	Activities							
1	*Call*	See 'General Strategies'							
1	Express Wants	1	11	44					
2	Direct Request	11	35	41	43	54			
2	Refuse or Disagree	5	7	22	28	38	46	49	52
2	Agree	5	7	22	28	38	46	49	52
2	Make Statement	27	38	39	47	51	53	54	
3	Express Feelings	20	23	27	46	48			
3	Express Attitudes	3	9						
3–7	Ask & Answer Wh Questions	13	25	29	31	42	52		
	(not How? or Why?)	19	26	30	37	45			
4	*Greeting*	See 'General Strategies'							
4	*Persist in Call*	15				+ see 'Strategies'			
4	*Request Repetition*	10		17	41	42	+ see 'Strategies'		
4	State Intention	18		19	21	36			
5	*Request Permission*	See 'General Strategies'							
5	Prohibition	18		19	20	25	51		
5	Give Explanation	7		16	25	37	45	47	49
6	Ask about Wants	2		12	44				
6	Ask about Intention	1		5	20				
6	*Offer*	2		44	+ see 'General Strategies'				
6	Make Suggestion	4		13	17	20	22	28	43
		6		15	19	21	24	33	
6	Ask Yes/No Question	6		11	13	14	15	20	25	32
6–7	*Give Clarification*	41		42	+ see 'General Strategies'				
7	Encourage	4		17	19	21	34	43	
7	Ask about Feelings	32		46	48				
7	Ask about Attitude	3		9	14				
7	Request Explanation (Why? How? and What for?)	7		16	23	37	46	49	
7/8	*Respond to Call*	See 'General Strategies'							
7/8	*Request Clarification*	11		41	42	+	see 'General Strategies'		
8	Make Generalisation	47							
8/9	*Check to confirm*	10		17	41	42	+	see 'General Strategies'	
9	Give Warning	18		19	20	28	35		
9	*Evasion*	22		+ see 'General Strategies'					
9	*Permit*	28		33	+ see 'General Strategies'				
9/10	*Promise*	See 'General Strategies'							
9/10	Challenge (+ Respond to Challenge)	17		20	24	33	50		
		18		21	28	35			
10	Make Condition	8		17	33	34	40		
10	Apologise	2		8	12	25	33		
10	Express Approval	4		7	19	24	50		
		5		12	21	28	52		
10	Express Disapproval or Criticise	4		5	7	12			

Note: Levels 1 → 10 indicate developmental progression (Gutfreund et al, 1989)

Activity Index Extension for negatives and questions

Activity Index Extension (optional) for work on Negatives

Level	Negatives	Activities							
DLS Levels 5–10	Refuse/Reject	5	19	24	51	53			
	Disagree	7	22	37	38	46	49	52	
	Prohibition	18	19	20	22	25	51		
	Inability	49	54						
	Denial	3	18	19	20	21	25	28	51 53

Source: based on Knowles and Masidlover, 1982; see also Gutfreund et al, 1989.

Activity Index Extension (optional) for work on the Development of Question forms

DLS Level	Questions	Activities						
5	What + do/doing/gone? e.g. 'What you doing?'	*						
5	Where + go/going/gone? e.g. 'Where you going?'	*						
6	Where/What + range of verbs e.g. 'What you eating?'	*	2	3				
6	Long Intonation questions for Yes/No Question – no inversion e.g. 'You going home now Ben?'	*						
7	Where/What + occasional auxiliary (no inversion) e.g. 'What you are doing?'	*	2					
7	Yes/No Question + Inversion e.g. 'Do you like it?'	6	7	11	14	20	25	32
8	Who?	6	23	25	31			
8	How?	46						
8	Why?	16	25					
8	Inversions + auxiliaries in Yes/No Questions							
8	'Have you got a . . .?'	6						
8	'Can I . . .?'	13	23	32				
8	'Am/Is/Are . . .?' 'Does it have a big . . .?'	13						
9	Question beginning with QW word and inverted auxiliary verb and subject e.g. 'What is that man making?'	12	13	14	46			
9	Inversion with some past auxiliaries e.g. 'Did he go to school?'	25						
9	Tags e.g. 'That's a helicopter isn't it?'							
10	When?	29	30	37	45			
10	What for?	13						
10	Whose?							
10	Which?	50						
10	How many/How much?	3	52					
10	Didn't he go to . . .?							

Note: *Where activities are not specified in the above table, use activities from higher developmental forms of related questions e.g. for Level 6 Long Intonation Yes/No Questions, use Level 7 Yes/No Question with Inversion activities – it's the same function.
Source: based on Knowles and Masidlover, 1982 – 'Grammar and Complex Sentence Stage' Levels 5–10.

Activity by age index

Activity Number	Activity	Foundation Stage	Key Stage 1	Key Stage 2	Key Stage 3
1	Maker	yes	yes	maybe	no?
2	Pairs	yes	yes	yes	yes?
3	Playdough Puzzle	yes	yes	no?	no
4	Race	no	yes	yes	yes
5	Let's Draw it	no	yes	yes	no
6	Pairs Also	yes	yes	yes	yes
7	What's This For?	no	yes	yes	yes
8	Make Me Happy	no	no?	yes	yes
9	You Like – I Like	yes	yes	yes	yes?
10	Memory Magic	yes	yes	yes	yes
11	Which One Do You Mean?	no	yes	yes	yes
12	Colour It Like This!	yes	yes	yes?	no
13	What's My Picture?	no?	yes	yes	yes
14	Ask Berty!	yes	yes	yes?	no
15	Musical Squares	yes	yes	yes	no
16	Go Together	yes	yes	yes	no?
17	Dice Deal	no	yes?	yes	yes
18	Joker!	yes	yes	yes	no?
19	Harvest Time	yes	yes	yes	no
20	Sharks!	yes	yes	yes	yes?
21	Target Practice	yes	yes	yes	yes
22	Mr Mix It Up	yes	yes	yes	no
23	Who–Di–Who?	yes	yes	yes	yes?
24	Suggest a Use	no	yes	yes	yes
25	Don't You Dare!	yes	yes	no?	no
26	Points For Pairs	no	yes	yes	yes
27	Story Time	yes	yes	yes?	no
28	Think About It!	no	yes?	yes	yes
29	When Can I Go?	no?	yes	yes	yes
30	Tell Me When	no	yes	yes	no
31	Who Has This?	yes	yes	yes	yes

Activity Number	Activity	Foundation Stage	Key Stage 1	Key Stage 2	Key Stage 3
32	Are You Feeling Happy?	no?	yes	yes	yes
33	Say It and Choose!	no?	yes	yes	yes
34	Get It and Go	no	yes	yes	yes
35	Build It High	yes	yes	no	no
36	I'm Going to Find It!	yes	yes	yes?	no
37	When Do You Need It?	yes	yes	yes	yes
38	That's Right . . . That's Wrong	no	no?	yes	yes
39	Say Something Different	yes	yes	yes	no?
40	A Bit Iffy	yes	yes	yes	yes?
41	Tell Me What To Do	yes	yes	yes	yes?
42	Ask Me What To Do	yes	yes	yes	no
43	Guided Walk	yes?	yes	yes	yes
44	Wanted!	yes	yes	yes	yes?
45	When Do You Do It?	no	yes	yes	yes
46	How Would You Feel?	no?	yes	yes	yes
47	All About This	yes	yes	yes	yes
48	Feely Pairs	no	yes	yes	yes
49	Can't Do It!	yes	yes	yes	yes
50	I Bet!	no?	yes	yes	yes
51	Won't Get Me!	yes?	yes	yes	yes
52	How Many Benny?	no?	yes	yes	yes
53	Silly Snacks	yes	yes	yes	yes?
54	No Can Do	yes	yes	yes	no?

Group plan sheet

'Chataway' Group Plan		
Group	**Date**	**Leader**
Resources *Warm up* *Activity 1* *Activity 2* *Other notes*		
Warm up		
Activity 1		
Activity 2		
Review of session		
Planning for next session		

Progress record

Level	Function	Children's names								
1	Call									
1	Express Wants									
2	Direct Request or Command									
2	Refuse or Disagree									
2	Agree									
2	Make Statement									
3	Express Feelings									
3	Express Attitudes									
3	Ask Wh Questions (**not** How? Why? or What for?)									
3–7	Answer Wh Questions (**not** How? Why? or What for?)									
4	Greetings									
4	Persist in Call									
4	Request Repetition									
4	State Intention									
5	Request Permission									
5	Prohibition									
5	Give Explanation									
6	Ask about Wants									
6	Ask about Intention									
6	Offer									

Chataway © Andrew Burnett and Jackie Wylie, Routledge, 2007

Progress record

Children's names

Level	Function								
6	Make Suggestion								
6	Ask Yes/No Question								
6–7	Give Clarification								
7	Encourage								
7	Ask about Feelings								
7	Ask about Attitude								
7	Request Explanation (Why?, How? and What for?)								
7/8	Respond to Call								
7/8	Request Clarification								
8	Make Generalisation								
8/9	Check to Confirm								
9	Give Warning								
9	Evasion								
9	Permit								
9/10	Promise								
9/10	Challenge (+ Respond to Challenge)								
10	Make Condition								
10	Apologise								
10	Express Approval								
10	Express Disapproval or Criticise								

Note: Levels 1 → 10 indicate a developmental progression
Source: Gutfreund et al, 1989

Chataway © Andrew Burnett and Jackie Wylie, Routledge, 2007

Progress record extension for negatives and questions

These two additional (optional) grids are for use where more detailed work is required to ensure satisfactory understanding and functional use of negatives and questions.

Progress record extension – negatives (optional)

Target												
Refuse/Reject												
Disagree												
Denial												
Prohibition												
Inability												

Children's names

Source: Knowles and Masidlover, 1982; Gutfreund et al, 1989.

Chataway © Andrew Burnett and Jackie Wylie, Routledge, 2007

Progress record extension – questions (optional)

Target	DLS Level*	Children's names							
What + do/doing/gone?, e.g. 'What you doing?'	5								
Where + go/going/gone?, e.g. 'Where you going?'	5								
Where/What + range of verbs, e.g. 'What you eating?', 'Where you running?'	6								
Long Intonation question for yes/no question – no inversion, e.g. 'You going home now Ben?'	6								
Where/What + occasional auxiliary (no inversion), e.g. 'What you are doing?'	7								
Yes/No Questions + inversion, e.g. 'Do you like it?'	7								
Who?	8								
How?	8								
Why?	8								
Inversions in Yes/No Questions + several auxiliary verbs, e.g. Have you got a . . .?	8								
Can I go to the. . .?	8								
Am/Is/Are?	8								
Does it have a big . . .?	8								
Questions beginning with a QW + inverted auxiliary and subject e.g. What is that man making?	9								
Inversions with some past auxiliary verbs e.g. Did he go to school?	9								
Tags e.g. That's a helicopter, isn't it?	9								
When?	10								
What for?	10								
Whose?	10								
Which?	10								
How many/How much?	10								
Negative Questions + QW and inversion e.g. Didn't he go to school?	10								

Source: based on the developmental progression in the DLS 'Grammar & Complex Sentence Stage' Levels 5–10; Knowles and Masidlover, 1982.

Note: DLS Levels 5–10 are *not* equivalent to the Chataway main Progress Record Levels 5–10; both classifications are, however, developmentally ordered.

Chataway © Andrew Burnett and Jackie Wylie, Routledge, 2007

CHAPTER 5

Activity Sheets (1–54)

Activities

1 Maker

2 Pairs

3 Playdough Puzzle

4 Race

5 Let's Draw It!

6 Pairs Also

7 'What's This For?'

8 Make Me Happy

9 You Like – I Like

10 Memory Magic

11 Which One Do You Mean?

12 Colour It Like This!

13 What's My Picture?

14 Ask Berty!

15 Musical Squares

16 Go Together

17 Dice Deal

18 Joker!

19 Harvest Time

20 Sharks!

21 Target Practice

22 Mr Mix It Up

23 Who-Di-Who?

24 Suggest a Use

25 Don't You Dare!

26 Points for Pairs

27 Story Time

28 Think About It!

29 When Can I Go?

30 Tell Me When

31 Who Has This?

32 Are You Feeling Happy?

33 Say It and Choose!

34 Get It and Go

35 Build It High

36 I'm Going to Find It!

37 When Do You Need It?

38 That's Right . . . That's Wrong

39 Say Something Different

40 A Bit Iffy

41 Tell Me What To Do

42 Ask Me What To Do

43 Guided Walk

44 Wanted!

45 When Do You Do It?

46 How Would You Feel?

47 All About This

48 Feely Pairs

49 Can't Do It!

50 I Bet!

51 Won't Get Me!

52 How Many Benny?

53 Silly Snacks

54 No Can Do

Learning goal:

Direct Request e.g. 'Make a snake'

Express Wants e.g. 'I want (you to make) a sausage'

Ask about Intention e.g. 'What car you gonna do?'

Make Statement e.g. 'That's a big plane'

1. Maker

You will need:

- Playdough or plasticine.

- Possibly some pictures illustrating things to make, e.g. sausages, man/woman, car, ring, letter shapes, general shapes, simple fruit shapes, snake, boat, plane – particularly useful for younger children.

Take turns to ask the rest of the group to make a shape.

The instruction can be simplified or complicated to suit the age and interests of the group.

The 'leader' can encourage discussion about people's models–

Make Statement or Ask about Intention e.g. 'What's yours going to be like Ben?'

 **Chataway**

2. Pairs

Learning goal:

Ask about Wants e.g. 'What do you need?', 'What you want?'

Express Wants e.g. 'I want a dog'

Apologise e.g. 'Sorry, not got that'

Offer/Ask Yes/No Question e.g. 'Here's a bird for someone'/'Anyone want a bird?'

You will need:

A pack of 'Pairs' cards e.g. Snap cards, or the 'MixPix' in the Appendix.

Mix the cards and deal four to each player.

Place the rest in a pile face down in the middle.

Players take turns to choose and then ask another person (Player 2) 'What do you need/want?'

Player 2 answers 'I want a dog' etc. The first player hands over the 'dog' card if they have it and player 2 then puts down the pair. Players replace used cards from the pile in the middle, until these are used up.

If Player 1 doesn't have the requested card they say 'Sorry, I can't help you!' or similar (**Apologise**). (Children like telling the other players they can't help!)

Player 2 then has to take a card from the middle pile instead. They offer it to the other players if they don't want/can't pair this card.

The next player then has a turn.

The player with the most pairs at the end of the game is the winner.

To play a similar game working on different language targets, see Activity 6 'Pairs Also'.

Chataway © Andrew Burnett and Jackie Wylie, Routledge, 2007

3. Playdough Puzzle

Learning goal:

Ask Wh Question (How Much?) e.g. 'How much I got?'

Answer Wh Question e.g. 'A big piece', 'Lots'

Make Statement e.g. 'I got loads'

Denial e.g. 'No, I got a little bit!'

You will need:

- Playdough or plasticine.
- Three cards – showing large, medium or small pieces.

While one player looks away/turns round/closes their eyes, the other players take turns to point to one of the three cards and the leader gives them an appropriate sized piece of the playdough.

When the one player opens their eyes the other players take turns to ask him/her, 'How much have I got?'.

The player gets a point for every correct guess or wins the lump of playdough/plasticine.

At the end of the game the player with the most points or dough gets a clap and the one with the least could be asked to 'entertain' the group with a song or similar.

Chataway © Andrew Burnett and Jackie Wylie, Routledge, 2007

Chataway

Learning goal:

Encourage e.g. 'Go on!', 'Try and get a 6!'

Express Approval e.g. 'Well done', 'That's good!', 'Nice one!'

Express Disapproval e.g. 'Oh no!', 'Only a 2!'

4. Race

You will need:

- A race 'track', dice and counters.
- Alternatively just use a dice, spinning top or numbers in a feely bag for the 'adding race'.

During an exciting 'race' track-based game involving two teams, use target phrases such as 'Go on Ben!' 'You can do it!' etc. (**Encourage**), and 'Brilliant Amy! (**Express Approval**), encouraging the other players to use similar phrases.

Copy and promote any words or phrases they use too.

At the end of the game you can also talk about particularly impressive moments e.g. 'when Ben got two sixes'.

A simpler version of this activity is to just roll a dice, use a number-based Spinning Top or take number cards/blocks out of a feely bag, and add up the team's score as you go along.

5. Let's Draw It!

Learning goal:

Suggestion e.g. 'Let's draw a car!'

Direct Request e.g. 'Draw a tree'

Express Approval e.g. 'That's nice'

Agree e.g. 'OK'

Refuse/Reject 'No, that's too hard'

Criticise e.g. 'Where are the windows?'

You will need:

- Paper, pencils.
- Ideas for pictures, if required.

Take turns in the group to suggest an item for all to draw.

Initially it is probably best to just work on this goal and then encourage the 'suggester' to comment on the group's efforts as they are drawing, or when they finish – model approval first, e.g. 'That's nice!', 'I like that', 'really good'.

If preferred you can encourage the speaker to give an instruction (**Direct Request**) instead of making a suggestion, a function which usually develops later.

Constructive criticism can be carefully included e.g. 'Where are the windows?' (re. car). Introduce it into to a group that is established and possibly incorporate it as part of a review of the work done.

NOTE – easy subjects are best, to help weaker artists, e.g. bus, flower, tree, cat, car, book, snake, clock.

6. Pairs Also

You will need:

A pack of 'Pairs' cards, e.g. animals, food, toys (Snap cards will usually be OK, or use the 'MixPix' set in the Appendix).

This is not a team game.

Shuffle the cards and deal out 3–5 per person (depends on the number of players), leaving some in the middle, face down.

Players take turns to ask another player, e.g. 'Have you got a frog?', trying to match a card they hold in their dealt hand.

Any pairs collected are placed on the table, following which the two players replace any used or donated cards with cards from the pile in the middle.

The person who asked the question usually has the next turn, but do remember to establish the rule that all players get a fair share of the turns.

Once the pack is used up, play continues until all the cards have been paired. The players then count their collection of pairs to see who has the most.

For a similar game, but with different language targets, see Activity 2 'Pairs'.

7. What's This For?

Learning goal:

Request Explanation e.g. 'What a kettle is used for'

Give Explanation e.g. 'A kettle is something you heat water in'

Agree/Disagree e.g. 'That's right'/ 'That's not right!'

Express Approval e.g. 'Good answer'

You will need:

Pictures of a range of objects, or the names of objects written on cards.

Some suggested items: kettle, hammer, fridge, umbrella, sellotape, PC, stamp, battery, welly boot, belt, laces, fork, traffic lights, stapler.

Take turns to pick a card/picture and then ask, for example, 'What is a fridge used for?'.

The person answering the question gives an explanation.

If the questioner accepts the explanation they give a 'point' (to the individual or other team). If the questioner disagrees with the answer, they can give their own answer and the group leader then decides who/which team should win the point.

The individual or team gaining the most points wins the game.

 Chataway

8. Make Me Happy

Learning goal:

Make Condition e.g. 'If you give me Mr Sole, I'll give you Master Pill' or 'We'll give you Master Pill if you give us Mr Sole' (harder)

Apologise e.g. 'Sorry, we haven't got it!'

You will need:

Card sets e.g. 'Happy Families'.

A rack for the team's cards, or a barrier.

Shuffle all the cards. Deal some for each team to share (they do not show them to the other team) and then place the remaining cards face down on the table.

Teams take turns to 'do deals' with the other team (Make Condition).

If Team 1 wants a card, e.g. Mr Sole, and Team 2 has it, Team 2 must pass it over.

Team 1 then puts the Sole family cards they now have face up on the table. Once this has happened Team 2 can't subsequently ask for Mr Sole or other cards in that set, e.g. Miss Sole.

If Team 2 can't help with e.g. the Mr Sole request, Team 1 is allowed to take a card from the pack on the table.

Players need to listen carefully because, for example, if they remember that Team 1 asked for Mr Sole earlier on in the game, they might pick up e.g. Mrs Sole during their turn – then they can collect the Sole family.

At the end of the game, the winning team will have the most pairs or sets.

Chataway © Andrew Burnett and Jackie Wylie, Routledge, 2007

Learning goal:

Ask about Attitude (Ask Yes/No Question) e.g. 'Do you like football?' or 'What sport do you like?'

Express Attitude e.g. 'I like sausages', 'I not like nothing'

9. You Like – I Like

You will need:

A prompt card or list with pictures or names of suitable topics – e.g., food, pets, sport, games, TV programmes, IT games, colours, drinks, toys (see Appendix for suitable category prompt cards).

Each person takes turns to ask the others in the group about their likes (and dislikes), using the picture prompts if required.

You can put the prompts (words and pictures) in one margin of a grid and the names of people on the other axis, setting up a proper investigation which can be continued with other people if required.

	Ben	Sarah	Amy	Gemma	Mr Smith
Sport					
Food					
TV Prog					
Pets					
IT game					

At the end you can encourage a discussion about shared likes and dislikes, e.g. 'We all liked pizza', 'Nobody liked pet snakes!'.

Learning goal:

Request Repetition e.g. 'Say it again please'

Check to Confirm e.g. '7349?'

Express Approval e.g. 'Well done', 'Brilliant!'

10. Memory Magic

You will need:

No equipment required.

Take turns to say a list of numbers e.g. '3–5–2', then ask another player to repeat this number string.

Once the task is established, increase to four numbers.

The listener is allowed to ask for one repetition before they respond.

You can also encourage players to **Check to Confirm** the information given before they respond.

Players also have three chances to ask a team member for help during the game – so everyone needs to be listening!

Adjust the numbers list to suit the group or individuals – raise or lower it as required. You could use names instead, e.g. 'sausage, apple, chips'.

Teams collect points for correct responses.

The leader could also give extra points to players who for example check and ask for repeats, or who help their team mates.

Learning goal:

Make Statement e.g. 'He's got red hair and he's wearing a . . .'

Express Wants e.g. 'I want the man with . . .'

Direct Request e.g. 'Give me the man with . . . please'

Ask Yes/No Question e.g. 'Have you got a lady with . . .?'

Request Clarification e.g. 'Which man do you mean?'

11. Which One Do You Mean?

You will need:

Card pairs where there are several similar pairs, e.g. 'Pairs' (Falcon Games) has cards depicting men and women with hats and other clothing – all slightly different. See also the Appendix 'Pairs' (note that these pictures can be expanded by colouring the same pair differently to make two pairs).

Game 1

Split the card pairs into two identical sets of single cards.

One set is displayed face up, the other set arranged in a pile, face down. Team members take turns to pick a card from the face down pile and they then describe the card, asking the other team to supply it from the face up display.

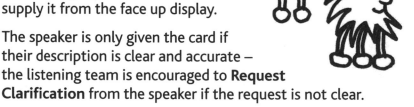

The speaker is only given the card if their description is clear and accurate – the listening team is encouraged to **Request Clarification** from the speaker if the request is not clear.

Game 2

Deal out the shuffled cards, leaving a few in a pile face down in the centre of the table.

Players take turns to ask other players for a card they want/need to make a pair. When cards are used to make pairs, the players take another card from the pack. Use **Requests for Clarification**, as described above. The winner has the most pairs.

12. Colour It Like This!

Learning goal:

Direct Request e.g. 'Do the chair brown'

Express Wants e.g. 'We need a brown (pen)'

Express Approval e.g. 'That's neat' 'That's like ours!'

Express Disapproval e.g. 'You went over the lines a bit'

You will need:

- Set of coloured drawings and same drawings without colouring.
- Felt tips/crayons and paper.
- A screen to visually separate the teams.

Provide a simple coloured drawing for Team 1 (or prepare a picture in advance), giving the same drawing, without colouring, to Team 2.

Team 1 also looks after the pens.

Team 1 members take turns to give colouring instructions and Team 2 will need to ask for the pens they need to do this.

The two teams should end up with pictures that look the same.

Team 1 can be encouraged to make positive comments about or constructive criticisms of Team 2's efforts.

If there is time, or the next time you use this activity, swap the team roles, i.e. give the prepared picture and pens to Team 2.

Picture preparation can in itself provide extended opportunities for language work – **Make Suggestion, Express Wants, Express Approval** for example.

 **Chataway**

Learning goal:

Ask Wh Questions e.g. 'What colour?' 'Where you find it?'

Ask Yes/No Question e.g. 'Is it large?'

Make Suggestion e.g. 'Ask him what group it's in'

Express Approval e.g. 'You guessed that quickly!', 'Well done'

13. What's My Picture?

You will need:

- A selection of picture cards, or written cue cards:

  Easy selection – ball, chair, dog, bus, banana etc.

  For older students – torch, pillow, rubbish bin, sink, lawn etc.

- 'Questions prompt card' if required (see Appendix).

For the team version one team member picks a card from the shuffled pack, taking care to only show it to his/her partners.

The other team's players take turns to ask questions about the picture, aiming to collectively work out what it is.

The team with the card can answer any questions but, if the questioners ask a direct question, e.g. 'Is it a banana?', that question counts as one of their team's three chances to identify the object. (For older students only allow 1–2 chances, as appropriate.)

Scoring – add up the number of questions asked by Team 2 and add that number to Team 1's score (and vice versa). This encourages players to listen to their team and think about the answers given.

At the end encourage **Approval** and other social language targets

You can use objects taken from a feely bag if preferred, or use items around the room, as in 'I Spy'.

Chataway © Andrew Burnett and Jackie Wylie, Routledge, 2007

 Chataway

14. Ask Berty!

Learning goal:

Ask about Attitude e.g. 'Do you like . . .'

Ask Wh Questions e.g. 'What food/games/colour do you like?'

You will need:

- Hand puppet, e.g. Berty.
- Prompt cards if required, e.g. Category Prompt Cards – see Appendix.

This is a useful activity for younger students.

The group leader can use the puppet initially, with group members taking turns to ask Berty what he likes.

It can help to provide suitable prompt cards, e.g. about colours, foods, games, sports, TV programmes, toys, etc. (also suitable questions to ask, or else model these clearly at the start).

You can extend the game to include what Berty doesn't like. See what the children can remember at the end of the game.

Who remembered the most?

Other players might also be allowed to 'look after' Berty and answer his questioners.

Chataway © Andrew Burnett and Jackie Wylie, Routledge, 2007

Learning goal:

Make Suggestion e.g. '(You could) Come on mine'

Offer e.g. 'You can come on mine Ben'

Persist in Call e.g. 'Ben! Ben!!! (Come on mine!)'

Ask Yes/No Question e.g. 'Can I come on your square please?'

15. Musical Squares

You will need:

Carpet squares – or big chairs, if they are tough enough!

This is a cooperative version of 'Musical Chairs' (inspired by Bill Harpe's *Games for the New Years*)

Spread the squares around the room and start to play a musical chairs style game, i.e. when the music stops, all players have to get on a square.

When the players resume moving round the room, remove a square.

When the music stops the second time players all have to find a square again – the key difference being that nobody is ever 'out' in this version of the game! So, naturally, players end up sharing squares – more each time you remove a square!

At the end of the game all players should be sharing one square and they have to have at least part of one foot on the final square – perhaps create a human sculpture which you could record on digital camera.

Good to promote cooperation and sharing.

The leader promotes the targeted language goals during the course of the game.

 **Chataway**

16. Go Together

Learning goal:

Request Explanation e.g. 'Why do these ones go together?'

Give Explanation e.g. 'Because they . . .'

You will need:

'Things that Go Together' cards LDA, or equivalent pictures or objects such as: key and lock, rubbish and bin bag, shoe and sock.

Split the card/object sets into two sets. A Team 1 player picks out a pair and asks a Team 2 player 'Why do these ones go together?' or a similar sentence.

The Team 2 player gives an explanation and if it is an acceptable answer Team 2 wins a point.

Alternatively, place all cards face down and play a more traditional game of 'Pairs'. If a player picks up a potential pair during their turn, the other team has to ask 'Why do they go together?'. If the player gives a good explanation, they win the pair and win a point for their team.

Older students might enjoy a more demanding version where they pick two cards randomly and have to explain how the things are linked, however different.

Extra points from the leader for imaginative ideas!

Chataway © Andrew Burnett and Jackie Wylie, Routledge, 2007

17. Dice Deal

Learning goal:

Make Condition e.g. 'If you get a 6, you can choose a card'

Encourage e.g. 'Go on Sophie, get a 6!'

Make Suggestion e.g. 'Let's ask if they will swap a card'

You will need:

Pack of cards including sets, e.g. 'Happy Families', and dice.

The aim for each team is to collect sets of cards.

Shuffle the cards and deal a few to each team, keeping the rest in a pile on the table, face down. The team put their cards face up on the table, with any part sets together e.g. part of a 'Happy Family'.

If Team 1 is due to start, a player from Team 2 can say, for example, 'If you roll a 3 or a 5, you can have a card'.

If the Team 1 player rolls a 3 or 5, they can take the top card from the pack on the table and add it to their collection.

If a 3 or 5 **isn't** rolled, Team 2 has its turn.

Each team will soon be able to start making up sets of cards from the ones they have collected. (Rule – if you are using 4-card sets, e.g. 'Happy Families', a team has priority in collecting that set if they already have two of the set.)

If one team has collected a card that is obviously wanted by the other team, the second team can **Make Condition**, at the same time trying to get a card that they want e.g. 'We will give you a . . . if you give us your . . .'

The team with the most sets of cards wins the game.

Chataway

18. Joker!

You will need:

Pack of playing cards, or a set of traditional 'Donkey' cards.

Using playing cards, select some of the cards e.g. all the 2s, 4s, 6s and one Joker. (Adjust number of cards to suit time available and also age of children – the more you have, the harder it is to find a given card.)

Spread out the cards face down on the table and mix them up ('swizzle').

On the first turn the player says 'I'm going to get a . . .'

If they choose the correct card, they keep it.

If it is a different card, it is returned to the table face down and the cards are given another 'swizzle'.

If a player picks the Joker (Donkey) all the other players say 'Uh-Oh!' ('Ee-orr').

The winner is the player (or the team) with the most cards.

Chataway © Andrew Burnett and Jackie Wylie, Routledge, 2007

Learning goals include:

Make Suggestion e.g. 'Try the cards in the big field'

Encourage e.g. 'Try and get a 6!'

Give Warning/Prohibition e.g. 'Don't get the Winter card!'

State Intention e.g. 'I'm going to get another food card'

Express Approval e.g. 'Well done Ben!'

Express Disapproval e.g. 'You got the Winter card!'

Denial/Reject e.g. 'You can't eat grass!', 'We don't want eggs'

19. Harvest Time

You will need:

- The 'Harvest Time' game set (see Appendix). Copy the game board onto A3 and colour. Make multiple copies of the food/animal cards and lotto boards.

- Dice and counters.

Shuffle the cards, then place a few cards, face down, on the 'fields' in the centre of the board.

The aim of the game is to fill the barn (lotto board) with food for people and animals, 'before the Winter comes'.

Players move around the board (playing in pairs), using a counter for each pair or individual.

When players land on a 'field' square, they can pick a card from one of the card piles in the 'fields' – don't get the Winter card!

Food/animal cards are placed in the barn.

Penalty cards direct players to put 1 or 2 cards back in the fields.

If someone picks up the Winter card before the barn is full, that is the end of the game – or start again (the players usually want to!).

20. Sharks!

Learning goal:

Express Feelings e.g. 'I'm scared'

Give Warning e.g. 'Look out Ben!'

Make Suggestion e.g. 'Shall we go the other way?'

Denial/Challenge e.g. 'You won't catch us Shark!'

Prohibition e.g. 'Don't go near the Shark!'

Ask Yes/No Question e.g. 'Is the treasure in the wreck?'

You will need:

- 'Sharks' game board and card set (see Appendix). Copy game board onto A3 size and colour. Make multiple copies of chance/treasure cards.

- Dice and counters (+ toy shark – optional)

The aim of the game is for the players to find the hidden treasure, avoid being caught by the Shark and get back to the boat.

The leader is usually 'The Shark' – a mostly non-speaking role.

The Shark starts in his cave and the other players start on the boat. The Shark secretly selects one of the treasure cards.

The players roll the dice in turns (working in pairs) and 'swim' to the different places around the board, looking for the treasure.

When they get to the places they can ask the Shark e.g. 'Is the treasure in the rocks?'.

If the Shark says 'No, it's not there' they carry on with the search.

If the treasure **is** there Shark gives them the treasure card and, using the dice, all the players try to get back to the boat without being caught by Shark.

Options:

If Shark lands on your square you can pick up a chance card (a mix of harpoons or Shark cards). If it's a harpoon, Shark has to move away 6 spaces. If it's a Shark card, he eats you!

Even if Shark does 'eat' a player, a popular option is for Shark to be so disgusted with how you taste that he spits you out and you end up back in the boat – you have to start again.

21. Target Practice

You will need:

- Five 'targets' boxes, numbered 1–5.
- Three bean bags.

The leader sets a target number for the teams – perhaps 30 for an initial practice run.

Each team player has three turns. They have to throw the bean bags so that they land in the boxes, scoring the appropriate number of points for their team.

Model the target language during the practice session.

Adjust the target number to suit the skill level of the group – and issue a challenge to them e.g. 'I bet you can't get more than 50!'.

Optional:

If the group doesn't reach the target number, they all have to do a forfeit. If they **do** reach it you, the leader, could do the forfeit (also optional, but popular)!

Forfeits could include: 5–10 press ups, hop around a table, sing a song, etc.

22. Mr Mix It Up

Learning goal:

Agree e.g. 'Yes', 'That right!'

Disagree e.g. 'No!', 'Wrong!'

Direct Request e.g. 'Do it right!'

Prohibition e.g. 'Don't say the wrong word!'

Make Statement e.g. 'You said plane instead of helicopter!'

You will need:

- Puppet.
- Objects or pictures – or just point to items around the room.

Younger children

Tell the group that Mr Mix It Up is good at naming things, but sometimes he mixes up the words. We need to help him get it right!

Start with a few correct references to items, e.g. 'That's a dog isn't it?!' → 'Yes'.

The children will enjoy correcting and helping Mr Mix It Up.

He could also model the use of **Evasion**, e.g. 'I don't know'.

Older students

Talking about topics, occasionally slipping in some incorrect information, can appeal to many older students. Award one point for each deliberate mistake identified – this could be done on a team basis.

Learning goal:

Ask Who Questions e.g. 'Who has the most . . .?'

Ask Yes/No Question e.g. 'Is it you?'

Answer Wh and Yes/No Questions

23. Who-Di-Who?

You will need:

A collection of small cubes – or number cards.

One person in the group closes their eyes while the others are given a number of the objects (1 to several) (or a number card), which they hide behind their backs.

The 'others' then say to the first player, 'Who has the most/highest number?' (or similar, to suit players' ages).

The first player has 1–3 guesses, winning 3, 2 or 1 point(s) as appropriate.

Players take turns to guess and try and win points.

You can also organise this activity to work as a team game.

Learning goal:

Make Suggestion e.g. 'It could be a shoe!'

Express Approval e.g. 'I like that idea!'

Challenge/Reject e.g. 'That can't be a shoe!'

24. Suggest a Use

You will need:

A variety of objects – choose objects which could be easily used for an imaginary use, e.g. 'hat' – could also be a bowl, a shoe, a cup, etc.; 'string' – could be spaghetti, a beard, a bird's nest, etc.

Put an object in the middle of the table and individuals make imaginative suggestions about how that object might be used.

You may need to model some examples first to encourage the children to think of uses away from the literal use of the object – e.g. a tennis racket could be a guitar or a big spoon, etc.

When the children make a suggestion they can then show the group how they would use it.

 Chataway

25. Don't You Dare!

Learning goal:

- **Prohibition** e.g. 'Don't touch my car!'
- **Ask Wh Questions** e.g. 'Who took my car?!', 'Why you do that?'
- **Ask Yes/No Questions** e.g. 'Have you got my bus?', 'Did you take my book?'
- **Denial** e.g. 'Not me!'
- **Apologise** e.g. 'Sorry Mr. Grumble'
- **Give Explanation** e.g. 'Cos I like it'

You will need:

- Mr Grumble puppet or alternative!
- Collection of pictures or objects.

Introduce Mr Grumble to the group and explain that he doesn't like people touching/playing with his things.

Mr G says 'Don't touch my toys please' or 'Don't touch my bus'.

While Mr G has a sleep one of the children is encouraged to pick one of his toys and show it to the others.

When Mr G starts to wake up, direct the child to hide the toy e.g. behind their back.

Mr G then questions the children in turn – make this a fun thing and they will enjoy it. The children deny responsibility or own up and apologise – Mr G always accepts the apology.

Continue with e.g. 'OK, you can touch my bus, but don't touch my train!!!'

Children can take turns to be Mr Grumble – or if it is easier or more manageable, they can take turns to 'look after' Mr Grumble's things when he is on his holidays! They can tell him all about what happened when he 'comes back'.

Chataway © Andrew Burnett and Jackie Wylie, Routledge, 2007

26. Points for Pairs

Learning goal:

Ask and Answer Wh Questions e.g. 'Who likes red?', 'How many sisters you got?', 'Which team do you support?'

Ask and Answer Yes/No Questions e.g. 'Have you got a cat?'

Make Condition e.g. 'If you have the same colour eyes you can put one in'

You will need:

Bean bags/balls or tokens of different colours for each player.

Players are given 5 bean bags/balls/tokens etc. Each player has a different colour.

The object of the game is to get as many of your tokens into the bucket as you can. You can only put a token in the bucket when you have found a partner.

The group leader starts by telling the group what partner they have to find, e.g.

'You can put a token in the bucket if . . . you find someone with the same number of brothers as you.'

'. . . you find someone who likes the same colour as you'.

'. . . you find someone who gets to school the same way you do'.

'. . . you find someone who has the same pet as you', etc.

Players have to move around the room asking others questions to find a person with the same answer as them. When they have found a partner they can come to the group leader who will check their answers and will then let them put a token into the bucket.

Older children could have the chance to be the leader and make the conditions. Conditions can also be more physically based, e.g. 'If you have the same size hands, the same colour eyes', etc.

Learning goal:

Make Statement e.g. 'The boy is trying to catch a ball'

Express Feelings e.g. 'I'm very angry now!'

27. Story Time

You will need:

Sets of sequenced story cards.

Ask the group to sort out the story cards in the correct sequence.

Children take turns to start/continue/end the story, talking about one card each. You will need to establish if it is a 'story' using the past tense, e.g. 'The girl went . . .' or a shared 'reading', e.g. 'I'm going out' said the girl.

Encourage a review of the story where feelings and reactions to the events can be discussed and formulated.

Extension activity:

A Role Play of the story provides a useful and popular follow-up activity for many younger children (especially Foundation up to Year 1).

If you use the Role Play option, leave the story sequence on view so that the children can refer to it if necessary. It's also useful and productive to get the children to swap parts and then re-tell the story.

28. Think About It!

Learning goal:

Challenge e.g. 'I bet it's a 5!'

Denial e.g. 'No it aint!', 'No, we've had that one already!'

Permit e.g. 'You can have a counter'

Express Approval e.g. 'Good guess!', 'Lucky!', etc

Give Warning e.g. 'Don't say 4 again!'

Make Suggestion e.g. 'Go on, say a 5'

You will need:

- Playing cards, as specified below.
- Counters (or a score sheet).

If there are six players, select all the number 2, 3, 4 and 5 cards i.e. 16 cards and shuffle them (adjust number of cards to suit the size of the group). Place the cards face down on the table.

Team 1 discusses their challenge and then one player says, e.g. 'I bet it's a 4' (from 2, 3, 4 or 5).

A player from Team 2 turns over the top card.

If the card is a 4, Team 2 says 'well done' etc. and 'permit', e.g. 'you can have a counter'.

If the card is not a 4, they say 'bad luck, good try' etc.

The used card is then put face up in the middle of the table, so all players can see it.

Teams take turns, always discussing their challenges as a team, i.e. suggesting, warning, etc.

You can help them predict what is likely to still be in the pile, e.g. 'If 3 × 5s have gone, what is likely to be left in the pile? Think about it and talk to your partners!'.

The winning team has the highest score/most counters.

Chataway © Andrew Burnett and Jackie Wylie, Routledge, 2007

29. When Can I Go?

Learning goal:

Ask When? Questions e.g. 'When can I colour in the next bit?'

Answer When Questions e.g. '(If) you get a six', '(When) you get a 3'

You will need:

- A beanbag + numbered targets.

- A black and white picture of a scene or something with clear sections, e.g. a house.

- Alternative activity – a track game + counters and a dice, or an obstacle course + a dice.

Activity 1

Team 1 player asks, 'When can I colour in the . . .?'

Team 2 identifies a target, e.g. 'If you score 6' (hitting it with the beanbag). Player hits target → colours in the specified part of the picture. If they miss, the next player asks their question, and so on.

Once Team 1's picture is completed the teams swap roles.

Activity 2

Using the track game, the Team 1 player asks 'When can I move?'

Team 2 player says, e.g. 'If you get a 3 or a 6'.

If successful, the Team 1 player can then roll the dice again and move their team counter towards the finish.

Teams take turns to ask the 'When?' questions.

 Chataway

30. Tell Me When

Learning goal:

Ask When? Questions e.g. 'When is your birthday?', 'When do you eat. . . .?'

Answer When? Questions e.g. 'July', 'In the morning'

You will need:

- A paper grid with children's names along one axis and question key words, e.g. 'birthday' along the other.

- Suitable topics include; birthday, bedtime, watch TV, eat dinner.

The leader starts by asking one of the group, e.g. 'When do you clean your teeth?'. Record the time, e.g. 8 o'clock, on the grid.

The person who answered can then ask someone else a question, the process continuing until the group's grid is full.

It will be helpful to have answer prompts available, e.g. names of months, food types, etc.

Extension activity

Discuss people's answers and note similarities and differences.

Learning goal:

Ask Who? Questions e.g. 'Who has green eyes?'

Answer Who? Questions e.g. 'I do.'

31. Who Has This?

You will need:

Some simple cue cards or written cues to include for example: green eyes, blue eyes, dark hair, brown shoes, a watch, a pet dog, two sisters.

Shuffle cue cards and place face down on the table.

Team 1 takes a card and asks the appropriate question, e.g. 'Who has a pet cat?'. Team 2 scores a point for every team member who can answer the question 'me'.

Team 2 takes a card and questions Team 1.

The team with the most points wins.

Alternatively make a collaborative grid of information to record who has what in the group, and review similarities/differences at the end.

Chataway

Learning goal:

Ask about Feelings e.g. 'Are you feeling worried?'

Ask Yes/No Questions e.g. 'Could it be frightened or scared?'

32. Are You Feeling Happy?

You will need:

'Emotions' cards set (see Appendix) or similar. (Older students can just have the words written on cards.)

Shuffle the cards and place face down on the table.

A Team 1 player picks a card and acts out the emotion displayed/written on the card.

Team 2 players try to guess what emotion is written on the card, but they must ask Team 1 a question like: 'Are you feeling frightened?'.

Team 2 is allowed three guesses and wins the card if correct. If they don't get the correct answer Team 1 keeps the card.

Teams take turns and the team with the most cards wins.

Chataway © Andrew Burnett and Jackie Wylie, Routledge, 2007

33. Say It and Choose!

You will need:

Pairs or card sets (use cards chosen by the students).

Teams will need to think up and discuss some tasks for the other team first – if necessary suggest football team players, types of car, pop star names etc. and write a list.

Deal out an equal number of cards to the two teams, leaving a few cards in an upside-down pile in the middle.

Team 1 makes the first condition, e.g. 'If you tell us the name of a Top Ten band, you can ask for a card'.

Team 2 responds to the request – perhaps after a team discussion? If correct, one of the Team 2 players is allowed to ask for a card that they are collecting, i.e. one of a pair, or one of a set they are collecting.

If Team 1 doesn't have the card requested, they apologise and allow (**Permit**) Team 2 to take a card from the pile on the table.

Team 2 can keep this card if they need it, but then have to put one card they don't want at the bottom of the pile.

Teams take turns and the team winning the most card sets wins the game.

Chataway © Andrew Burnett and Jackie Wylie, Routledge, 2007

Chataway

Learning goals:

Make Condition e.g. 'If you've got an 8, you can roll the dice'

Make Suggestion e.g. 'We've got some 8s – say 8!!'

34. Get It and Go

You will need:

- A pack of playing cards (or other card sets if preferred).
- A dice.

Shuffle the cards and deal a few to each player, leaving enough to have a 'pack' of cards face down on the table.

A Team 1 player makes a condition for Team 2 (see example).

If somebody on Team 2 can put **one** of the specified cards down, they are allowed to roll the dice. The number rolled is then added to the Team 2's score sheet.

The teams take turns to make conditions and put down cards/roll the dice, adding to their scores as appropriate.

Teams pick up cards from the pack to replace those they have put down. Once the pack is used up, end the game.

Players can whisper suggestions to their team, e.g. suggesting cards they as a team mostly hold – which the other team therefore probably haven't got! (Encourage tactics!)

The team with the most points at the end of the game wins.

Chataway © Andrew Burnett and Jackie Wylie, Routledge, 2007

Learning goal:

Direct Request e.g. 'Put a green one on next'

Challenge e.g. 'I bet you can't build a tower of 12 bricks!'

Give Warning e.g. 'You'll make it fall!'

35. Build It High

You will need:

Coloured wooden cubes or equivalent materials.

Team 1 tells players from Team 2 which colour brick to add next when building a tower.

The leader keeps a note of how many bricks are added before the tower eventually falls down.

When that happens the teams change roles with Team 2 now 'giving the orders'.

The winning team is the one which either builds the tallest tower or which uses the greatest number of bricks.

Further challenges or, hopefully, congratulations are possible here.

36. I'm Going to Find It!

Learning goal:

State Intention e.g. 'I'm going to find a . . .'

You will need:

A set of cards or objects that interest the students.

All the players look at and name the collection of cards/objects.

Whilst Team 1 players turn their backs or close their eyes a Team 2 player takes one item and holds it behind their back.

A player from Team 1 then identifies which item has gone e.g. 'fish'.

Next, they say 'I'm going to find the . . . fish', at the same time pointing at the Team 2 player they think has hidden the fish. (If necessary, allow younger players to make 1→3 guesses.)

If their guess is correct, players win a point for their team.

Chataway © Andrew Burnett and Jackie Wylie, Routledge, 2007

75

Learning goal:

Ask When? Questions e.g. 'When do you need an umbrella?'

Answer When? Questions e.g. 'When raining'

Agree/Disagree/Make Suggestion

37. When Do You Need It?

You will need:

- Pictures of everyday objects which are used for specific purposes at specific times, e.g. umbrella, bed, knife, scissors, sellotape, spoon, coat, screwdriver, hammer etc.

- A simple race track style game board, dice and counters.

Play this game in teams or as individuals.

Place the picture cards in a pile face down on the table.

To roll the dice and move along the race-track players first need to correctly answer a 'When?' question.

The 'When?' question can either be asked by the group leader or an opposing player/team (depending on their level of ability).

The person asking the question picks up a picture card and asks a 'When?' question relating to that picture, e.g. 'When do you need a hammer?', 'When do you use a spoon?'.

Another team or player answers the question. This can give rise to some general discussion about whether the answer is correct. Opposing teams/players may like to suggest alternative correct answers, e.g. 'No it's not that . . . you need it when you're tired' etc.

38. That's Right . . . That's Wrong

Learning goal:

Agree e.g. 'Yes', 'That's right'

Disagree e.g. 'No!', 'Wrong!', 'That's not right!'

You will need:

You may carry out this activity with no written prompts but you may find it easier to have a prepared list of statements/sums.

Your prepared statements or sums will be a mixture of correct and incorrect, e.g. 'dogs are always black', 'grass is always green', '2+2 = 5', '3+1= 4', 'snakes never have legs', 'it always snows in the winter' etc.

Make sure that your statements match the ability level of the children you are working with.

Older children can read the statements to the group themselves. Younger children will need the group leader to read them.

If the children are in teams they can discuss this together and work out if they agree or disagree with the statement/sum.

Such discussion may introduce other Chataway goals such as **Requesting Clarification** e.g. 'What do you mean?'; **Making Generalisations** e.g. 'Snakes don't have legs'; and **Giving Explanations** e.g. 'Cos some are brown' and so on.

Learning goal:

Make Statement e.g. 'The girl is sitting under the chair'

39. Say Something Different

You will need:

A composite picture with plenty going on in it for the children to talk about.

Ask the group to take turns to say something about the picture. They have to make one statement and then pass the picture on to the next person. They are not allowed to repeat what anyone else has said.

This activity could be extended to include statements about how the characters in the pictures are feeling.

If there is any repetition the group may need to be encouraged to use other Chataway skills such as **Disagreeing and Giving Explanations**, e.g. 'No, cos Ben said that' or **Making a Suggestion**, e.g. 'Say tree falling down!'.

Chataway © Andrew Burnett and Jackie Wylie, Routledge, 2007

Learning goal:

Make Condition

e.g. 'If you are wearing blue socks, stand up'

e.g. (harder) 'Stand up if you are wearing blue socks'

40. A Bit Iffy

You will need:

- For older children – no materials needed.

- If playing with younger children, you may want to use picture prompt cards to represent the 'if . . .' and the 'then . . .' (e.g. a picture of blue socks and picture of someone jumping → 'If you are wearing blue socks, jump up and down' etc.).

This is rather like a 'Simon Says' type activity – useful after a table-top based activity.

After the leader has modelled a few conditions and instructions, the children take turns to think up sentences to say to the rest of the group, e.g. 'If you have long hair, put your hand up', 'If you are wearing black shoes, hop to the door' etc.

Younger children will need help to formulate these instructions, and you could use picture prompts or gesture to encourage and assist them.

Help the children to formulate their ideas as well as they can, e.g. 'You got blue jumper, you jump'.

41. Tell Me What To Do

Learning goals:

Direct Request e.g. 'Put the red brick on top of the yellow one', 'Put the duck behind the tractor'

Check to Confirm e.g. 'The yellow one?', 'Behind the tractor?'

Request Repetition e.g. 'Say that again please'

Request Clarification e.g. 'The blue one or the yellow one?', 'The bike or the tractor?'

Give Clarification e.g. 'The blue one I said', 'The duck'

You will need:

- Two identical sets of building bricks (e.g. Lego).
- Or two identical sets of toys (e.g. farmyard).
- A barrier to go between the teams or individuals.

Work in two teams or pairs. Sit opposite sides of the table and put up a barrier between the teams or players (e.g. prop up some books or files). The object of this 'barrier' game is for both sides to end up with the same model or layout of toys by describing what they have done so the other side can do the same.

One side starts by building something with their bricks or putting their toys in different places. They then have to describe/explain what the other side needs to do by giving a direct request, e.g. 'Put the big yellow brick on top of the little blue one', 'Put the little pig in the field'. The other side may need to ask questions or request clarification to help them understand.

Compare models/toys at the end and talk about where it went well (i.e. where the models/toys are exactly the same) and where it went wrong (i.e. where the models/toys differ in some way). When finished swap roles so that the other team/individual makes a model/arranges their toys and then gives instructions to the first team.

Learning goal:

Ask Wh Questions e.g. 'What colour?', 'Where do it go?' etc.

Answer Wh Questions

Check to Confirm e.g. 'Next to the tractor?'

Request Repetition e.g. 'Can you say that again?'

Request Clarification e.g. 'The big one or the little one?'

Give Clarification e.g. 'The big one'

Make Statement e.g. 'That like our picture!'

42. Ask Me What To Do

You will need:

- Two identical black and white pictures and a set of colouring pens/two identical re-useable sticker sets.

- A barrier to go between the teams or individuals.

Work in two teams. Seat the teams on opposite sides of a table and put up a barrier between them (e.g. prop up some books or cardboard). The object of this 'barrier' game is for both sides to end up with the same picture by describing what they have done so the other side can do the same.

In this version of the game the emphasis is on one side asking the other side questions to get helpful information.

One side starts by colouring part of their picture or putting a sticker in a specific place, etc. The other side then has to ask questions to find out what that team has done so that they can do the same, e.g. 'What colour did you use?', 'What did you colour?', 'What sticker did you put on?', 'Where did you put it?' etc.

They will also need to ask questions to check and clarify, e.g. 'Big or little?', 'Where did you say?', 'Next to the car?' etc.

Take turns to colour in/stick and ask questions. When the pictures are finished compare and talk about them.

Chataway © Andrew Burnett and Jackie Wylie, Routledge, 2007

43. Guided Walk

You will need:

A blindfold, a beanbag, a box or bin and some obstacles to get around, e.g. skittles, plus 'route markers' e.g. a table, chairs.

Players can be divided into teams. The object of the game is to get your blindfolded team member to drop the beanbag successfully in the box/bin – don't make it a race as this tends to reduce the language level and raise the noise level!

Teams take it in turns and can be timed, or given points for avoiding the skittles, etc., by the group leader.

One team member is blindfolded. The team then has to give instructions to the blindfolded person to guide them round the obstacles. You may specify a particular course, e.g. they have to guide them over a table, under a chair and through a hoop. Arrange the course to suit the abilities of the children.

Encourage individuals in the teams to discuss what they are going to get him/her to do next before giving the instruction, e.g. 'Why don't we get him to go forward?', 'How many steps do you think he'll need to take?', etc. Team members can make 'suggestions' and 'agree' or 'disagree' with suggestions that others make.

Encourage the team to give their blindfolded team member lots of praise and encouragement.

Chataway © Andrew Burnett and Jackie Wylie, Routledge, 2007

 Chataway

44. Wanted!

Learning goal:

Express Wants e.g. 'I want a 4', '(I need a) Lion!'

Offer e.g. 'You can have this 3', 'Have this lion'

You will need:

- A set of cards – e.g. paired number or animal cards.
- Optional – Noah's Ark picture/number lotto board.

If using number cards, shuffle the cards and deal out one to each player, encouraging them to keep their card secret – it might be a good idea to put cards in pockets! The leader keeps the remaining cards to distribute later in the game.

Encourage one player to say what they want/need, e.g. 'I need a 6'. They choose another player and ask, e.g. 'Have you got a 6?'.

If yes, the two players take their pair to the leader and collect two new 'secret' cards.

If Player 2 answers no, another player with that card can *offer* it to Player 1. Players 1 and 3 then take the pair to the leader and collect new cards.

If there is no pair card in play for Player 1, Player 2 takes the next turn.

Eventually all the cards will be paired.

To make this more attractive for the younger players, the leader could have a Noah's Ark for animals or a lotto board for numbers.

Chataway © Andrew Burnett and Jackie Wylie, Routledge, 2007

45. When Do You Do It?

Learning goal:

Ask When? Questions e.g. 'When do you . . . go to bed/watch TV?', etc.

Answer When? Questions e.g. 'At 9 o'clock'

Agree/Disagree e.g. 'You don't watch telly at 10 o'clock!'

You will need:

- A set of **'time' cards** marked 3, 6, 10 o'clock, etc. – these could be in the form of clock pictures, or written times with added symbols to clarify the time of day.

- A set of **'event' cards** (pictorial or written cues), e.g. TV, bed, bath, meals, school, swimming.

Shuffle the cards and deal out one 'event' card to each player in Team 1 and one 'time' card to each player in Team 2.

Team 1 players take turns to ask 'When do you . . .?' and Team 2 members put their hand up if they think their card shows an appropriate time for the activity.

Correct answers earn a point for the team and players from both teams are dealt a new card after their turns.

Some answers generate discussion and disagreement, e.g. do people watch TV before school?

Finish after a set number of turns. Collect all the cards, reshuffle the two sets and then deal the 'time' cards to Team 1 and 'event' cards to Team 2, enabling a role swap.

46. How Would You Feel?

Learning goal:

Ask about Feelings e.g. 'How would you feel if someone spilt your drink?

Express Feelings e.g. 'I would feel angry'

Request Explanation e.g. 'What would you do if . . .?'

Agree/Disagree e.g. 'Me too', 'No, I'd shout at him!'

You will need:

'Emotions' cards set (see Appendix), or similar.

Shuffle the cards and place them face down in the centre of the table.

One player in the group takes a card, looks at the illustration (e.g. ripped book) and asks someone else in the group, e.g. 'How would you feel if someone ripped your book?'.

The chosen person explains how they would feel.

The leader can extend this exchange by opening the discussion up to other group members, to see if they would feel the same or possibly respond in a different way – a useful opportunity to encourage extended discussion.

Players may offer alternative words, e.g. 'angry' → 'mad', 'upset'.

They may disagree, or use personal examples, or imagine how they would react in a similar situation.

It can be useful to write down keywords, perhaps also adding symbols to help the players remember and reflect on the discussion.

Chataway © Andrew Burnett and Jackie Wylie, Routledge, 2007

Learning goal:

Make Statement e.g. 'It's very soft'

Give Explanation e.g. 'You can use it for a game'

Make Generalisation e.g. 'They are always bouncy'

47. All About This

You will need:

- A variety of objects or pictures, e.g. ball, other toys, box, hat, crayon, rubber, cup, tin opener, etc.

- Encourage the children to collect the items – they will then definitely want to talk about them!

This activity works well in an informal circle time setup.

Whoever is 'ready' selects the first item from the pile in the centre of the circle and says one thing about it.

They then pass the item clockwise and the next person has to say something different. This progresses round the circle – several times if people continue to come up with new ideas.

The leader may need to recap what has already been said if the children start to repeat earlier contributions.

For groups who find it hard to think of new ideas or are a bit quiet you could have a practice round, with leader prompts for colour, shape, size, etc.

You could also use a prompt card + symbols for younger players.

Chataway © Andrew Burnett and Jackie Wylie, Routledge, 2007

48. Feely Pairs

Learning goal:

Ask about Feelings e.g. 'How does he feel?', 'How this one feel?'

Express Feelings e.g. 'That makes him feel angry', 'He happy'

You will need:

'Emotions' cards set (see Appendix) or similar (see below regarding card selection).

This is a pairs game to be played as individuals or in teams.

Select picture pairs for the game where the situations would result in the same or a similar emotion, e.g. hugging a friend and going swimming etc.

Mix the pictures and lay them face down on the table.

A Team 1 player turns over two pictures. A player from Team 2 then asks them about the pictures they have chosen, e.g. 'How would you feel if this happened?', 'How he feel?'

If the emotions could be the same for each picture then Team 1 wins the picture pair and has another turn. If not the pictures are returned face down, the cards are mixed and a Team 2 player has a turn.

The leader might have to make a judgement if there is a disagreement – they can also award 'bonus points' for teams that use interesting emotional vocabulary i.e. not just 'happy' and 'sad'.

Chataway © Andrew Burnett and Jackie Wylie, Routledge, 2007

49. Can't Do It!

Learning goal:

Express Inability e.g. 'He can't run', 'He no fly', 'Not jump'

Ask and Answer Why Questions e.g. 'Why can't he jump?', 'Because he's got no legs'

Agree/Disagree e.g. 'You're right!', 'No he can't!'

You will need:

- Pictures of animals/characters either real or made up (e.g. aliens and monsters).
- Dice.
- Game board (optional).

Put the pictures of characters/animals face down in the middle of the table. You can play this game in two teams or as individuals. Players take turns to choose a picture and tell the group something that that character can't do, e.g. 'He can't jump', 'Can't eat', etc.

If others agree with them they can then throw the dice to collect points or move round a game board. To make this harder for older children they have to throw the dice first and then think of that number of things that the character can't do before moving (e.g. throw a 4 and think of 4 things, etc.).

You can extend this activity to include asking and answering 'Why?' Questions, e.g. one team asks the other 'Why can't he eat chewy sweets?' and the other team has to respond appropriately, e.g. 'Cos he's got no teeth'. Some ideas may prompt agreement/disagreement between teams and individuals.

Learning goal:

Challenge e.g. 'I bet you haven't got a 7!', 'You not got lion!'

Respond to Challenge e.g. 'Yes we have!'

Express Approval e.g. 'Well done Ben!'

50. I Bet!

You will need:

- Playing cards (use two of each numbered card + picture cards) or equivalent 'Pairs' cards.
- Score sheet.

The leader shuffles the pack and deals out some cards to all the players, keeping a few of the cards.

After discussing plans with their team, Team 1's first player challenges the other team, e.g. 'I bet you haven't got a King!'.

If the other team **doesn't** have a card to match this, the first team scores the points.

If the other team **does** have a matching card, they put it down and 'cancel' the bet – 'Yes we have!'

Teams take turns, with the leader keeping the score.

Scoring

Playing cards – score reference the card number, with 10 for picture cards.

'Pairs' cards – use the same points for all cards.

Tip for younger players – teams share cards, using one card rack.

Older students – use three cards per number/picture card. If teams match the challenge with the other two cards, they can win 10 bonus points!

Chataway © Andrew Burnett and Jackie Wylie, Routledge, 2007

Learning goal:

Denial (also *Challenge*) e.g. 'You won't get me out!', 'No Way!'

Prohibition e.g. 'Don't give me the same one!'

Rejection e.g. 'I don't want the same card!'

Make Statement e.g. 'I bet Jamie gets it!'

51. Won't Get Me!

You will need:

Pack of playing cards.

If you have eight players, sort out two sets of the same eight cards, e.g. 2–9 or 7–Ace inclusive. Shuffle one set, keeping it face down and then add one extra 'secret' card from the second set.

Before you deal out one card, face up, to each player you can set up the denials and challenges regarding which two players are likely to get the same card (e.g. 'I think I'll get you out this time'/'No way Miss!', etc. When two players are dealt matching cards they are 'out'.

After this first round, take out the paired card and reshuffle the pack of eight cards, adding a different unseen pair card.

Continue this process until you have 1–2 players left who have not been dealt a paired card. 'Well done – we never got you out!'

There is a small chance that you will not deal out the paired card – 'Miss, you didn't get any of us that time!'

 **Chataway**

Learning goal:

Ask Questions (How many?) e.g. 'How many have I got?'

Agree/Disagree e.g. 'That right!', 'No!!!'

Express Approval (or Regret) e.g. 'Good guess!', 'Well done!', 'Bad luck!'

52. How Many Benny?

You will need:

Cards with a number 1–5 written on them, or use playing cards. Arrange to have at least two cards for each number.

Shuffle and then deal out one card to each of the Team 1 players.

The Team 1 players take turns to ask Team 2 'How many have I got?'.

Team 2 discusses and then guesses 'how many'. If they have guessed correctly they win the card. If not, Team 1 wins the card.

When all the players in Team 1 have asked their question, the teams add up the numbers on the cards they have won.

Reshuffle the cards and deal out one each to the Team 2 players, repeating the process as outlined above.

You can also play this game with children taking turns to be asked 'How many?' by all the other players (deal a new card to all the players for each round).

At the end of the game, the team or individual with the most points wins. Follow this with a round of congratulations and commiserations!

Learning goal:

Denial e.g. 'You can't eat socks!'

Rejection e.g. 'I not eat grass!'

Make Statement e.g. 'I like sausages'

53. Silly Snacks

You will need:

- A selection of pictures of food items, plus pictures of non-edible things such as socks, pencils, hats – OR a selection of objects in a feely bag.

- For younger players, one bingo board for each team.

Shuffle the picture set and place face down in the centre of the table.

Players take turns to pick up a card and decide if they can/will 'eat' the item – if they can/will they keep the card (yum, I like sausages!) – placing it on the bingo board if used.

If they reject the card they are encouraged to say 'You can't . . .' or 'I not like/eat . . .'. And then put the card in the 'finished' pile.

First team to get a target number of cards or fill their bingo board wins.

Plenty of opportunities for the leader to encourage discussion about why people do/do not eat some things, e.g. salad.

Also some fun discussions possible when a player picks up a card of something they can't eat such as an old sock, dog biscuit, etc.!

Learning goal:

Inability e.g. 'I can't do that'

Make Statement e.g. 'I can!'

Direct Request e.g. 'Touch your knees'

54. No Can Do

You will need:

Ideas for or lists of actions that children can and can't do, e.g. touch their toes/nose/back, touch the ceiling, do a forward roll, make a body star shape, sing a high/low note, say a nursery rhyme, etc.

The leader says 'let's see if we can touch our nose'.

Leader does it and says, 'I can', encouraging the children to say something similar, e.g. 'I can', 'me too', 'me do it!'.

When suggesting a difficult task say, 'I can't do this!' and exaggerate your inability.

Always make sure that all the children CAN do at least some of the actions and also suggest some that you the leader can't do! (this will be a popular move and the children will either say 'I can't' but some children may well be able to show off their skills, e.g. touching toes!).

Children will be keen to take turns to lead in this game (it works rather like 'Simon Says').

Resources and Bibliography

Resources recommended for Activity Sheets

- Playing Cards
- 'Pairs' Cards, e.g. Snap, Donkey
- 'Happy Families' card set
- Playdough, Plasticine
- A selection of 'track' games
- Dice and counters
- Paper, pencils, crayons or felt tips
- A selection of common objects
- Picture cards depicting common objects
- Hand puppet
- Carpet squares
- 'Things that Go Together' card set (LDA)
- Feely Bag
- Boxes to provide 'targets'
- Beanbags
- A collection of maths cubes or cards with written numbers
- Story sequencing cards (everyday sequences of events)
- A selection of picture scenes, in black and white + a coloured version
- Simple cue cards
- Wooden cubes or equivalent
- Composite action pictures
- Blindfold
- 'Obstacles'
- 'Time' and 'Event' card set
- Pictures of food and drink items

Links to useful resources

Falcon Games – playing cards, especially 'Happy Families', 'Donkey', 'Pairs' and 'Snap' – available from a variety of High Street and other retail outlets.

The Green Board Game Company www.greenboardgames.com – 'Jungle Snap' and 'Happy Families' – available from a variety of retail sources.

Taskmaster – blank playing cards (using permanent marker pens to produce durable playing cards).

Big Leap Press – www.bigleapdesigns.co.uk for some great game boards.

Wendy Rinaldi – Social Use of Language Programme (SULP) Story packs 1–3. www.wendyrinaldi.com

Writing with Symbols 2000 – Widgit Literacy Symbols (previously Rebus), Widgit Software Ltd., www.widgit.com

Sources of other functional language activities and ideas

Brandes, D. and Phillips, H. (1977) *Gamester's Handbook*. Cheltenham: Stanley Thornes (Publishers) Ltd

Brandes, D. (1982) *Gamesters' Handbook Two*. Cheltenham: Stanley Thornes (Publishers) Ltd

Bond, T. (1986) *Games for Social and Life Skills*. London: Hutchinson

Delamain, C. and Spring, J. (2004) *Understanding and Using Spoken Language*. Bicester: Speechmark

Dynes, R. (2000) *The Non-Competitive Activity Book*. Bicester: Speechmark

Greenwood, J. (1997) *Activity Box – a resource book for teachers of young students*. Cambridge: Cambridge University Press

Hadfield, J. (1984) *Elementary Communication Games*. Harlow: Longman

Harpe, B. (2001) *Games for the New Years*. Liverpool: The Blackie

Knowles, W. and Masidlover, M. (1982) *The Derbyshire Language Scheme*. Derby: Derbyshire County Council

Lee, W.R. (1979) *Language Teaching Games and Contests*. Oxford: Oxford University Press

Locke, A. and Beech, M. (1991) *Teaching Talking*. Windsor: NFER-Nelson

Palim, J. and Power, P. (1990) *Jamboree*. Walton-on-Thames: Nelson

Qualifications and Curriculum Authority (2003) Primary National Strategy *Speaking, Listening and Learning: working with children in Key Stages 1 and 2*. DFES Publications

Tough, J. (1981) *A Place for Talk*. London: Ward Lock Educational

Wright, A., Betteridge, D. and Buckby, M. (1984) *Games for Language Learning* (new edition). Cambridge: Cambridge University Press

Selected Bibliography

Knowles, W. and Masidlover, M. (1982) *The Derbyshire Language Scheme*. Derby: Derbyshire County Council

Gutfreund, M., Harrison, M. and Wells, G. (1989) *Bristol Language Development Scales*. Windsor: NFER-Nelson

Hadfield, J. (1984) *Elementary Communication Games*. London: Longman

Harpe, B. (2001) *Games for the New Years*. Liverpool: The Blackie

Johnson, M. (2005) *Functional Language in the Classroom* (3rd. edn).

Locke, A. and Beech, M. (1991) *Teaching Talking*. Windsor: NFER-Nelson

Qualifications and Curriculum Authority (2003) Primary National Strategy Speaking, Listening and Learning: working with children in Key Stages 1 and 2. DFES Publications

Tough, J. (1981) *A Place for Talk*. London: Ward Lock Educational

Appendix: game cards

1. 'Sharks' board game plus game cards
2. 'Harvest Time' board game plus game cards
3. People Pairs cards
4. 'MixPix' cards
5. Emotions game cards
6. Category prompt cards
7. Questions prompt cards (including Rebus Symbols)

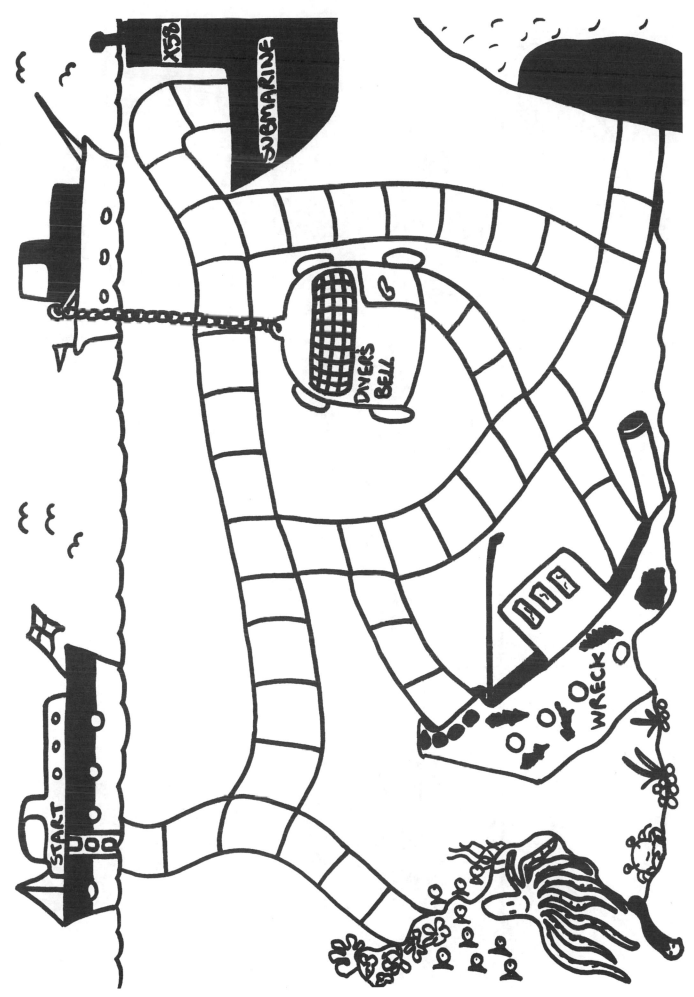

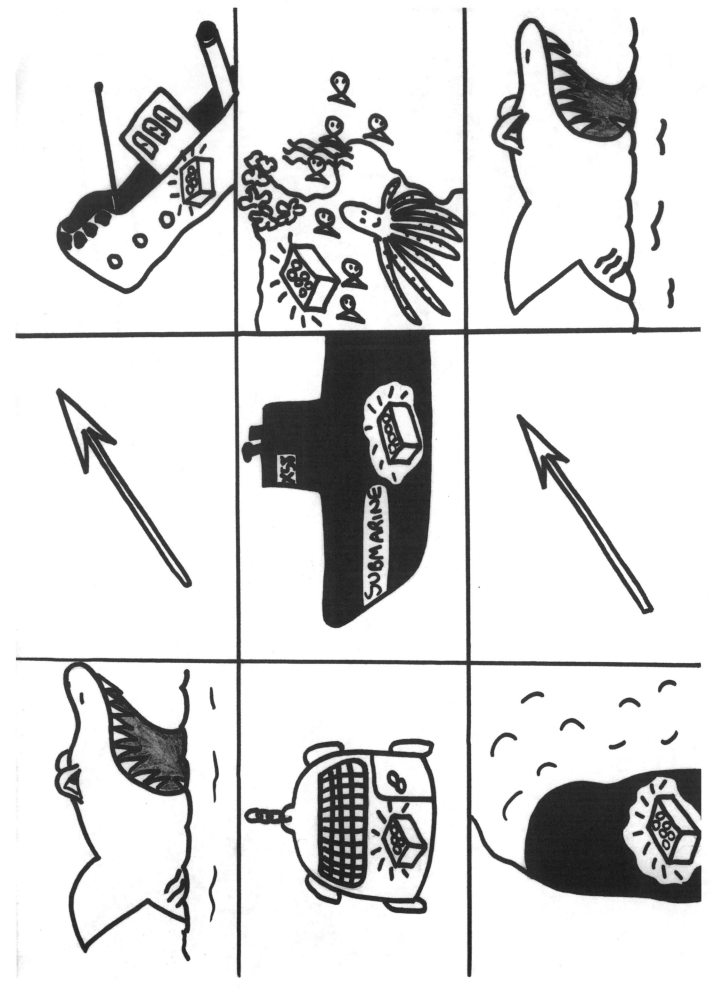

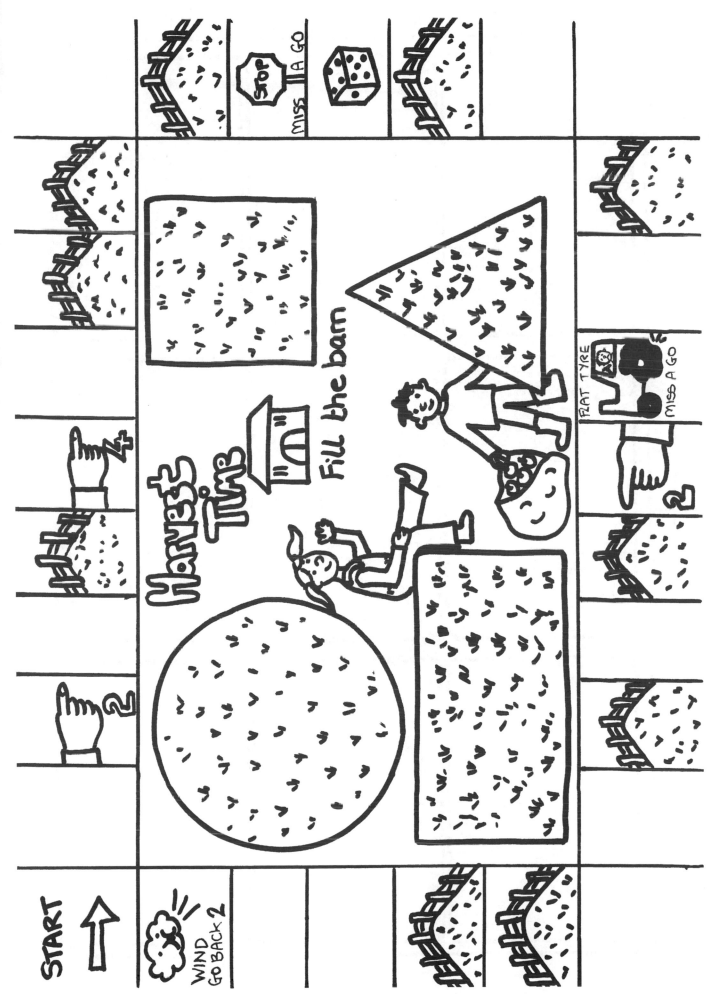

Harvest Time

Fill the barn

STOP
MISS A GO

FLAT TYRE
MISS A GO

START

WIND
GO BACK 2

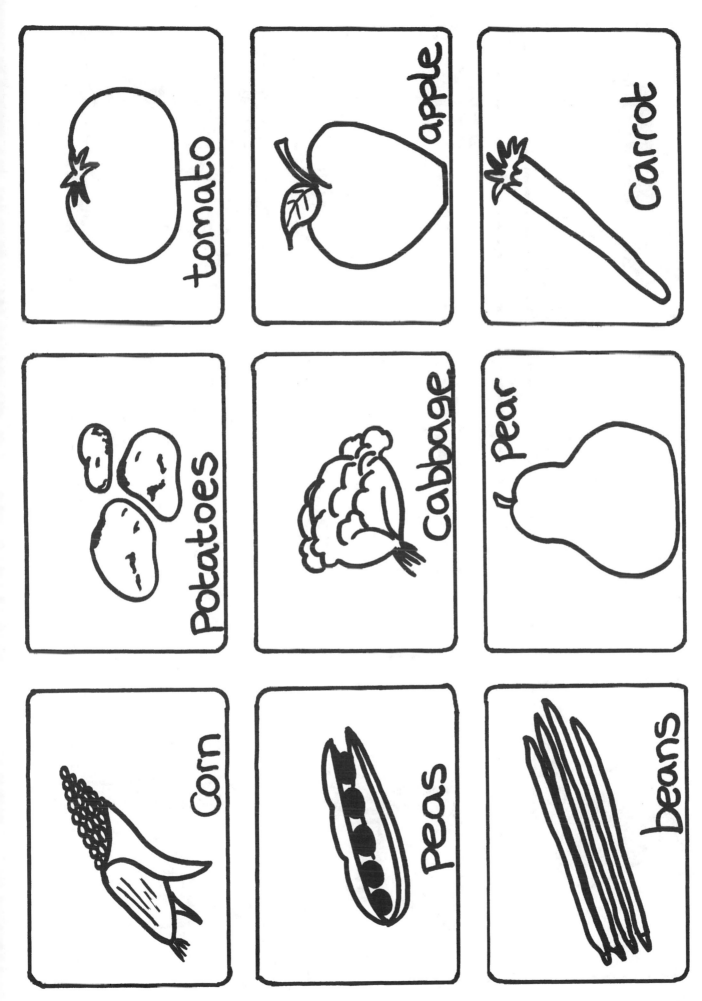

Chataway © Andrew Burnett and Jackie Wylie, Routledge, 2007

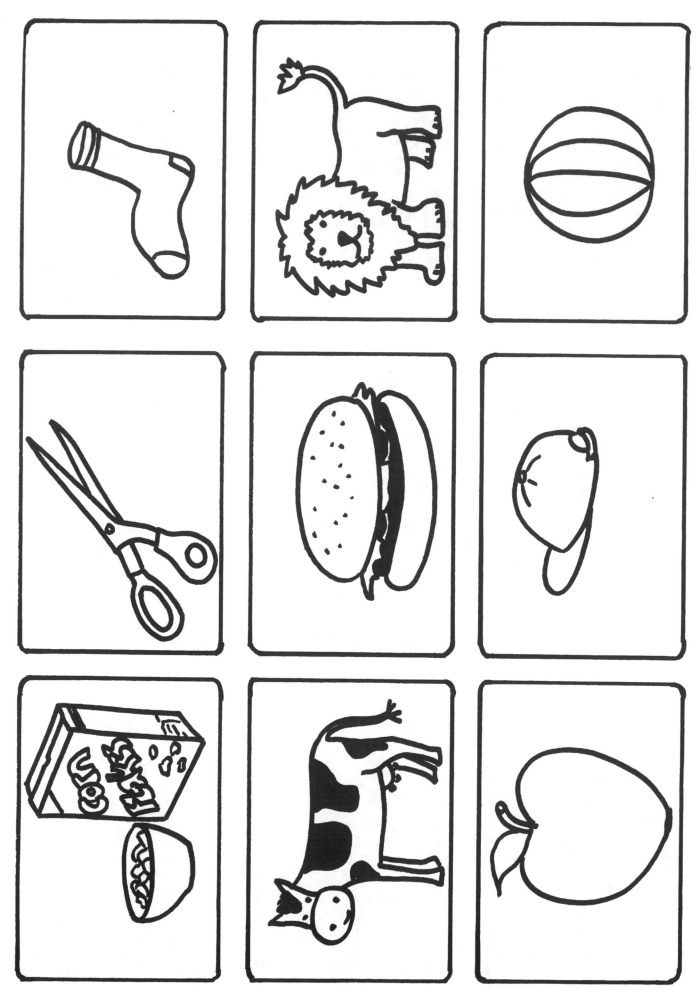

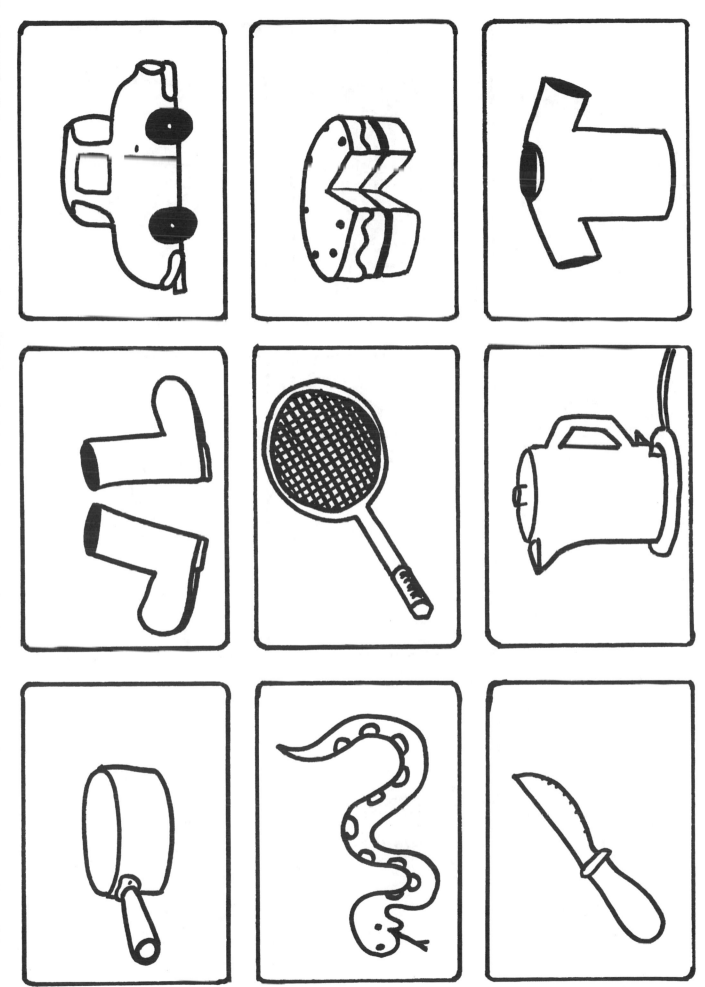

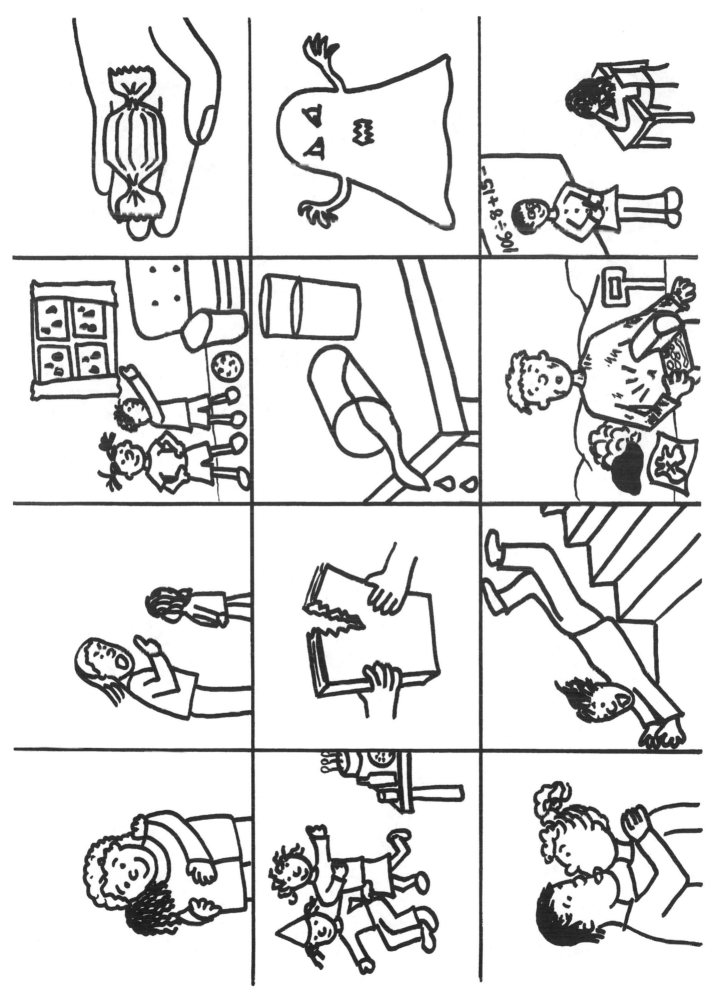

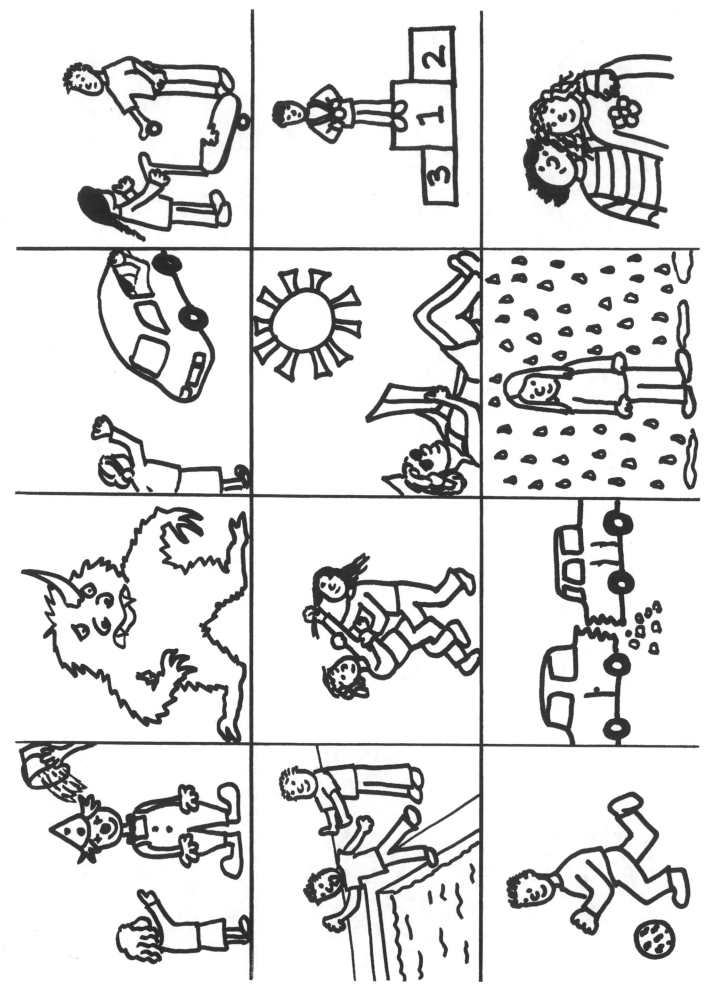

Band

Game

TV

Subject

Sport

Holiday

Food

Drink

Chataway © Andrew Burnett and Jackie Wylie, Routledge, 2007

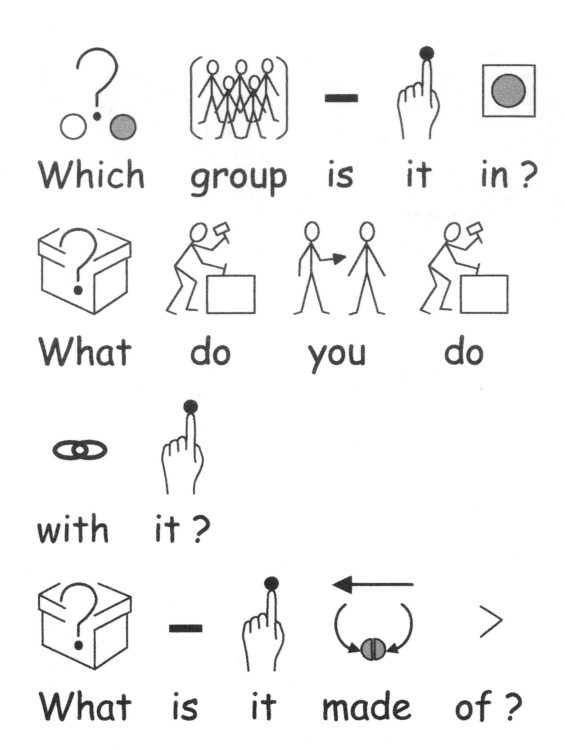

Which group is it in?

What do you do

with it?

What is it made of?

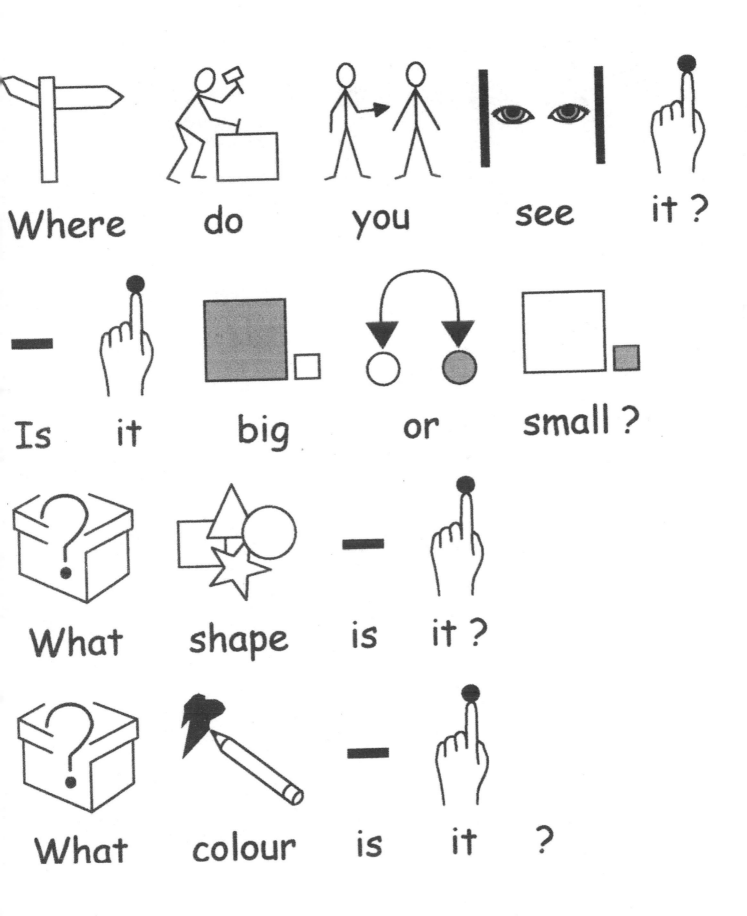

Where do you see it ?

Is it big or small ?

What shape is it ?

What colour is it ?

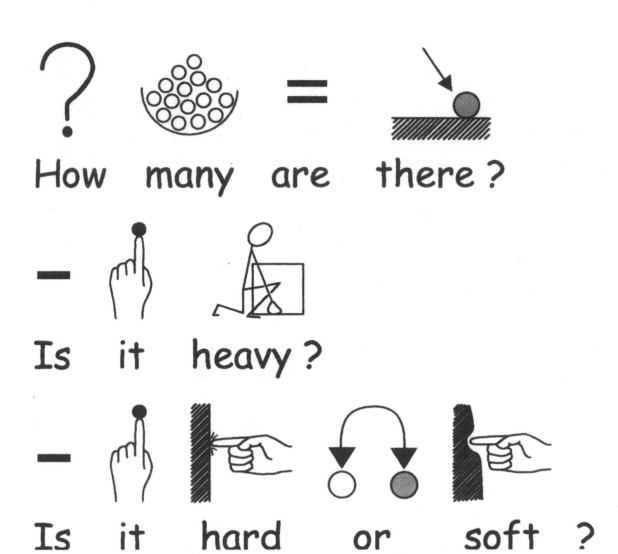

How many are there ?

– Is it heavy ?

– Is it hard or soft ?

6031